NOTTING HILL GATE
3

Herausgegeben von
Dr. phil. h. c. Christoph Edelhoff, StD a. D., und
Prof. Dr. phil. Torben Schmidt, Leuphana Universität
Lüneburg, Mitglied THE ENGLISH ACADEMY

Erarbeitet von
Denise Arrandale (Neumünster), Michael Biermann
(Hamburg), Hannelore Debus (Mörfelden-Walldorf),
Susanne Quandt (Bremen)

sowie
Otfried Börner (Hamburg), Pamela Hanus (Hamburg),
Ingrid Preedy (Dortmund), Kathleen Unterspann
(Halstenbek), Jürgen Wrobel (Oberursel)

Fachliche Beratung
Lieselotte Bohnsack (Essen), Rolf-Olaf Geisler
(Oberhausen), Dr. Sandra Götz (Gießen),
Semra Siyli (Hamburg), Dr. Ivo Steininger (Wetzlar)

Diesterweg
westermann

NOTTING HILL GATE 3

Für Klasse 7 an Gesamtschulen und anderen integrierenden Schulformen

Materialien für Schülerinnen und Schüler

- Textbook 978-3-425-14003-2
- Workbook mit Lernsoftware und Audio-CD 978-3-425-14023-0
- Klassenarbeitstrainer 978-3-425-13963-0
- Lernsoftware Einzelplatzlizenz 978-3-425-14053-7
- Westermann Vokabeltrainer-App www.westermann.de/vokabeltrainer
- Inklusions- und Fördermaterialien mit Audio-CD 978-3-425-14673-7

Materialien für Lehrkräfte

- Lehrerfassung zum Schülerband 978-3-425-13993-7
- Teacher's Manual 978-3-425-14803-8
- Vorschläge für Lernerfolgskontrollen mit CD-ROM 978-3-425-14843-4
- Workbook mit Lösungen und Audio-CD 978-3-425-14813-7
- Audio-CD für Lehrkräfte 978-3-425-14833-5
- DVD für Lehrkräfte 978-3-425-14823-6
- Kopiervorlagen 978-3-425-14853-3
- Lernsoftware Schullizenz 978-3-425-14883-0

Vorbereiten. Organisieren. Durchführen.
BiBox ist das umfassende Digitalpaket zu diesem Lehrwerk mit zahlreichen Materialien und dem digitalen Schulbuch. Für Lehrkräfte und für Schülerinnen und Schüler sind verschiedene Lizenzen verfügbar. Nähere Informationen unter **www.bibox.schule**

Diagnostizieren. Fördern. Evaluieren.
Die OnlineDiagnose zu diesem Lehrwerk testet die wichtigsten Kompetenzen und erstellt individuelle Fördermaterialien und Arbeitshefte zum Downloaden oder Bestellen. Nähere Informationen unter **www.onlinediagnose.de**

westermann GRUPPE

Druck A[6] / Jahr 2022
Alle Drucke der Serie A sind im Unterricht parallel verwendbar.

Redaktion: Redaktionsbüro Sabina Piatzer (Hannover) sowie Jutta Eckardt-Scheurig, Stevan Veljkovic und Daniel Walker
Illustrationen: Ulf Marckwort, Kassel
Umschlaggestaltung: blum design und kommunikation, Hamburg
Umschlagfoto: Dirk Schmidt/dsphotos.de
Layout: tiff.any GmbH, Berlin
Druck und Bindung: Westermann Druck GmbH, Georg-Westermann-Allee 66, 38104 Braunschweig

ISBN 978-3-425-**14013**-1

Inhalt

In diesem Workbook findest du folgende Symbole:

A1 Diese Aufgabe gehört zum **Basisweg**.

A7 Diese Aufgabe gehört nicht zum Basisweg und ist **fakultativ**.

CD 1/15 Der Hörtext ist auf den **Audio-CDs** für Lehrkräfte.

CD 127 Der Hörtext ist auf der **Audio-CD** für Schülerinnen und Schüler.

DVD 4 Der Videoclip ist auf der **DVD** für Lehrkräfte.

Zu dieser Aufgabe gibt es einen Videoclip.

LiF p. 130 1 Hierzu gibt es eine Erklärung im Grammatikteil ***Language in Focus*** hinten in diesem Workbook.

leichte Aufgabe

mittelschwere Aufgabe

schwierige Aufgabe

A8 Choose
Sucht euch eine Aufgabe aus. Ihr könnt allein arbeiten, zu zweit oder in einer Gruppe. Ihr könnt euch auch eine eigene Aufgabe ausdenken.

A9 Target task
Unterstützung für die Zielaufgabe der Sequenz

how to listen TB p. 143 Hierzu gibt es eine Erklärung auf den ***How to …***-Seiten im Textbook.

wordbank events TB p. 159 In den ***Wordbanks*** im Textbook finden sich die wichtigsten Wörter zu einem Thema.

model text Ein ***model text*** ist eine Vorlage für deinen eigenen Text.

Diese Aufgabe eignet sich für die kooperative Arbeit in der Klasse mit allen Schülerinnen und Schülern.

Can you remember?

Answer the questions and find out how much you remember from last year.

1. Who met a dog in the fog?
   - Charlie and Lisa ☐
   - David and his parents ☐
   - Vanessa and her dad ☐

2. Where is Mount Snowdon?
   - in Wales ☐
   - in Scotland ☐
   - in Northern Ireland ☐

3. Which animal escaped from London Zoo?
   - a lion ☐
   - a gorilla ☐
   - a tiger ☐

4. Who played fortune-tellers?
   - Gillian and Vanessa ☐
   - Gillian and Karla ☐
   - Gillian and David ☐

5. Who hated Robin Hood?
   - an old farmer ☐
   - the King of England ☐
   - the Sheriff of Nottingham ☐

6. Which festival is on 5 November?
   - Halloween ☐
   - Bonfire Night ☐
   - Chinese New Year ☐

7. What is 26 December called in Britain?
   - Boxing Day ☐
   - Boxers' Day ☐
   - Christmas Day ☐

8. What was Gillian's birthday surprise for her mum?
   - A nice dinner ☐
   - A surprise party with a lot of people ☐
   - A bottle of perfume from Selfridges ☐

9. Who had chickenpox?
   - Charlie ☐
   - Rajiv ☐
   - David ☐

10. Who sent a music request to DJ Rasta?
    - Karla and Gillian ☐
    - Karla and Vanessa ☐
    - Gillian and Vanessa ☐

A1 Lots of good food

CD 1

a) Listen to Claire and Leo. What do they want to eat?

Claire wants to eat ______________________________

Leo ______________________________

b) Write down more words for the food and the things in the picture.

____

____

____

____

____

____

c) Compare your list with a partner.

d) If you could choose food from this buffet, what would you eat? Talk to your partner.

First I would eat ... and then ...

I would eat ... because I like ...

... looks delicious. I think I would take a lot of that.

...

A2 How does it taste?

a) Write down two or three foods or drinks for each adjective. Use a dictionary.

wordbank food and drink TB p. 158

bitter: ____________________ savoury: ____________________

crispy: ____________________ sour: ____________________

crunchy: ____________________ sweet: ____________________

hot: ____________________ tasty: ____________________

b) Compare your lists in class. Make a wordbank together.

A3 A menu

a) 'The Green' is a new restaurant. The menu is still empty. You can decide on the choice of dishes and drinks. Complete the menu the way you like it best.

Roast chicken • Cheesecake • Cheese and chilli naan • Water • Thai red curry • Cream of tomato soup • Ice tea • Lemon pie • Beef and onion pie • Chips • Fried mozzarella balls • Potatoes • Chicken burger • Onion bread • Soft drinks • Broccoli curry • Rice • Juice • Bread pudding • Shoulder of lamb • Lemonade • Garden salad • Fruit sorbet • Tea or coffee • Fresh fruit plate • Green beans • ...

b) Add the prices for the dishes. Look at TB A3 for ideas.

c) Talk to a partner. Compare your dishes, drinks and prices.

Tipp
Ihr könnt die Speisekarte bei der Bearbeitung von TB A11 verwenden.

I chose ... and ... for starters. What about you?

How much are the desserts on your menu?

Starters

____________________ ______

____________________ ______

Main courses

____________________ ______

____________________ ______

____________________ ______

____________________ ______

Side dishes

____________________ ______

____________________ ______

____________________ ______

Desserts

____________________ ______

____________________ ______

____________________ ______

Drinks

____________________ ______

____________________ ______

A4 In a restaurant

a) Listen to TB A4 again and number the pictures in the right order.

CD 1/1 2

b) Listen again and write down the people's dishes and drinks.

c) Write W for 'waiter/waitress' and G for 'guest' next to the speech bubbles.

- Excuse me, could we have the bill, please?
- What are you having?
- Certainly, madam. And for you, sir?
- Good evening. Are you ready to order?
- Let me pay for today's lunch.
- OK, what shall we have?
- What's your food like?
- That's £19 altogether, please.
- Certainly, sir. Anything else?

Tipp
Du kannst TB A3 zu Hilfe nehmen, wenn du unsicher bist, wie man die Namen der Gerichte schreibt.

Work with a partner or in groups of three. Make up another short dialogue for one of the restaurants from TB A3 and act it out.

A5 Before and after eating

a) What can the waitress and the guests say in these situations? Complete the dialogues. Look at TB A7 for help.

wordbank food and drink TB p. 158

Dialogue 1: Before eating

Waitress: ____________________

Pam: Yes, I'd like the vegetable lasagna, please.

Waitress: Certainly. ____________________

____

Michael: I'll have spaghetti bolognese and a side dish of olives, please.

Waitress: ____________________

____

Pam: A bottle of water, please.

Waitress: ____________________

____

Dialogue 2: After eating

Waitress: So how was everything?

Michael: It was really delicious, thanks.

Waitress: I'm glad you enjoyed it. Would you like some dessert?

Pam: No, thank you. Can we ____________________

____

Waitress: Yes, ____________________

____

Michael: Thanks for the lovely dinner, Pam.

____

____

Pam: You're welcome. I really enjoyed it, too.

b) Find more phrases in TB A4 and A7 that waiters/waitresses and guests use before and after eating. Make two lists like this in your vocab folder:

before eating	
waiter/waitress	guest
...	...

after eating	
waiter/waitress	guest
...	...

A6 Say it in English

Write down phrases you can use in a British restaurant. Look at TB A7 for help.

1. Wie fragst du, ob ein Gericht mit Kartoffeln serviert wird?

____

2. Wie sagst du, dass du nicht zu viele Pilze und zu viel Schinken haben möchtest?

____

3. Wie sagst du jemandem, er solle sein Portmonee wegstecken, weil du zahlen willst?

____

4. Wie fragst du englische Freunde, ob ihr aufbrechen wollt?

____

A7 At an Indian restaurant

a) You are in London with your aunt and you go to an Indian restaurant. Your aunt does not understand English very well. Help her to order a meal.

Waiter: Hello, are you ready to order?

You: Weißt du schon, ______

Your aunt: Nein, ich verstehe vieles auf der Karte nicht. Kann er uns etwas empfehlen?

how to mediate TB p. 145

You: My aunt ______

Waiter: Yes, of course. Chicken tikka masala is very popular. It's chicken with spices in a creamy tomato sauce.

You: ______

______

Your aunt: Ist es sehr scharf?

You: ______

Waiter: No, it's not very hot. I can ask the cook to make it extra mild.

You: ______

Your aunt: Oh, wie nett. Ja, dann nehme ich das.

You: ______

Waiter: And what about you, what would you like?

You: ______

Waiter: Very good. And what would you like to drink?

You: ______

Your aunt: Ich hätte gern Mango Lassi. Bestell dir bitte, was du gern magst.

You: ______

Waiter: Thanks, I'll be back in a minute with your drinks.

b) Compare your dialogues in groups of three. Decide on one version. Then read it out.

A8 Much or many?

a) Complete the sentences with 'much' or 'many'.

1. There are ______________ nice restaurants in Notting Hill.
2. Are there ______________ curry houses near Portobello Road?
3. How ______________ garlic naan should we order?
4. Gillian doesn't eat ______________ meat because she is a vegetarian most of the time.
5. Rajiv likes vegetables, but he doesn't eat as ______________ carrots as Gillian.
6. How ______________ different herbs does Rajiv use for his curry?
7. Don't eat too ______________ ice cream – you might get stomach ache.
8. How ______________ did Gwen pay for the meal?

LiF p. 130 1

CD 4

b) Listen to the CD and check your sentences.

Cross out the wrong words. Be careful: sometimes both words are correct.

1. I'm really full. I've eaten so many/much chips.
2. There are many/a lot of curry dishes on this menu.
3. You should eat a lot of/lots of salad. It's good for you.
4. How many/How much fish and chips shops are there in your area?
5. There is a lot of/lots of cheese in the garlic and cheese mushrooms.
6. My sister and I don't drink much/many juice.

A9 Sound check

CD 5

a) Listen to the words and repeat them.

fantastic • typical • popular • delicious • available • recipe • savoury • selection • organic • recommend • average • opening • disgusting

b) Which words are stressed on the first syllable like 'typical'? Which words are stressed on the second syllable like 'fantastic'? Fill in the lists.

CD 6

c) Listen to the CD and check your lists.

Which word is stressed differently? Write down the word and where it is stressed.

____

____

stress on the first syllable	stress on the second syllable
typical	fantastic

A10 Have you ever …?

a) Write your name in the grid. Then answer the questions. Tick what you have done.

Have you ever …	your name:	name:	name:	name:
eaten a vegan burger?				
made pizza yourself?				
cooked a meal for a friend?				
tried tomato and avocado salad?				

LiF p. 130 2R

b) Add at least two interesting questions. Then interview three classmates.

c) Present some results to the class.

Have you ever …?

Yes, I have.

No, I haven't.

Yes, a few times.

Yes, but only once.

No, never.

…

A11 Choose

1. Make a list of five meat dishes, five fish dishes, five vegetarian dishes and five desserts.
2. Write about your favourite place to eat.
   - What is the name of the place?
   - Where is it?
   - What kind of food can you eat there?
   - What is your favourite meal there?
   - Why do you like it?
3. Write about a funny or a strange situation in a restaurant, for example when you get the dessert before the starter. Describe your reaction, too.

model text

My favourite place to eat is Asia House. It is on Höhenweg, near the planetarium. They serve Chinese food there. My family and I sometimes go there at the weekend. The restaurant looks nice because they have got lots of Chinese lanterns and paintings.
My favourite meal is chop suey. It is a dish with meat, different Asian vegetables and soy sauce. I think it tastes delicious.
Asia House is a great place because the food is really good and the waiters are very friendly.

how to write a rewiew TB p. 151

B1 At Rajiv's house

Who is it? Look at TB B1 again and tick the right names.

Who …	Rajiv	Gillian	Karla	Charlie	Vanessa
1. asks "How many onions do we need?"	☐	☐	☐	☐	☐
2. helps with the plaster?	☐	☐	☐	☐	☐
3. gives Karla the chilli paste?	☐	☐	☐	☐	☐
4. tells Gillian to have milk instead of water?	☐	☐	☐	☐	☐
5. says "It's worse than bad!"?	☐	☐	☐	☐	☐
6. likes the spicy curry?	☐	☐	☐	☐	☐

how to read TB p.144

Look at TB B1 again. Then close your book and tick the right endings.

1. Rajiv and his friends are making …
   - ☐ a curry and a banana raita.
   - ☐ a curry and a banana cake.
   - ☐ a curry and banana lassi.

2. They are also trying out …
   - ☐ Rajiv's grandmother's samosa recipe.
   - ☐ lots of new spices.
   - ☐ a new samosa recipe.

3. The friends want to raise money …
   - ☐ for a sports club.
   - ☐ for Notting Hill Carnival.
   - ☐ for charity.

4. Vanessa needs …
   - ☐ a plaster.
   - ☐ a handkerchief.
   - ☐ some water.

5. Karla uses …
   - ☐ two teaspoons of chilli paste.
   - ☐ two tablespoons of chilli paste.
   - ☐ four teaspoons of chilli paste.

6. Charlie tells Gillian …
   - ☐ to drink milk instead of water.
   - ☐ to drink water instead of milk.
   - ☐ to drink raita instead of water.

a) Look at TB B1 again. Then close your book and tick right or wrong.

	right	wrong
1. Rajiv has invited three friends for an Indian meal.	☐	☐
2. They are making curry, banana lassi and samosas.	☐	☐
3. They want to raise money for charity at Notting Hill Carnival.	☐	☐
4. Rajiv always makes curry the way his grandmother did.	☐	☐
5. Vanessa's eyes water because she has cut her finger.	☐	☐
6. Charlie tells Gillian to drink some milk instead of water.	☐	☐
7. Karla puts two teaspoons of sweet chilli sauce in the curry.	☐	☐
8. Rajiv tells his dad that Karla, Gillian and Charlie can't eat the curry.	☐	☐

b) Correct the wrong sentences in your exercise book.

B2 Money for charity

CD 1/7

a) Listen to TB B2 again. What charity does Rajiv want to raise money for?

____

b) Rajiv wants to sell samosas. What other things can you sell for charity? Where can you sell them? What charities can you raise money for? Add some ideas to the list.

Tipp
Benutze ein Wörterbuch.

things you can sell	place	charity or purpose[1]

[1] purpose – *hier: Zweck*

c) Compare your ideas in class. What are your favourite ideas?

d) Could you imagine selling food or other things for charity? Why or why not?

B3 You can do it, can't you?

a) Add the question tags.

aren't they • can't you • isn't he • hasn't she • haven't you • doesn't it • doesn't she • doesn't he • don't you

LiF p. 131 3

1. Rajiv is a great cook, ______________________________?
2. He cooks the way his grandmother did, ______________________________?
3. Karla and Rajiv, you really like the spicy curry, ______________________________?
4. Hot curry burns your mouth, ______________________________?
5. You have got quite a lot of spices in your cupboard, ______________________________?
6. Samosas are typical Indian food, ______________________________?
7. Rajiv's grandmother has got lots of good recipes, ______________________________?
8. You can find lots of curry recipes on the Internet, ______________________________?
9. Mrs Patel has a good idea how to make the curry less spicy, ______________________________?

b) Listen to the CD and check your question tags.

CD 10

B4 How to make vegetable curry

a) Read the recipe and number the pictures in the right order. Try to understand new words with the help of the pictures.

Tipp
1 tbsp.
= 1 tablespoon

1. Cut an onion and cook it in 1 tbsp. of oil.
2. Add 2 tbsp. of curry paste.
3. Add 400 g of canned tomatoes and 1 bag of frozen mixed vegetables.
4. Add 200 ml of water and cook the curry slowly for 15–20 minutes until the vegetables are well done.
5. Season the dish with salt and pepper.
6. Serve it with rice.

how to mediate TB p.145

b) Talk to a partner in German. Explain how to make vegetable curry.

B5 Little words

a) Fill in the right words.

about • around • for • in • onto • out • with

Remus: Would you like to come over ______________ dinner at the weekend? Diane and Cameron are going to come, too.

Phyllis: Oh, I'd love to. I enjoy having a nice meal ______________ friends.

Remus: I'm going to try ______________ a new chicken curry recipe. You rub a mix of yoghurt, garam masala, ginger paste and garlic paste ______________ the chicken pieces.

Phyllis: That sounds delicious. I have no idea ______________ typical Indian food.

Remus: Well, most people just buy curry powder[1] at the supermarket and put it ______________ their curry. But you can make it more interesting with other spices.

Phyllis: Great. I like tasting dishes from all ______________ the world.

CD 13

b) Listen to the CD and check your dialogue.

[1] curry powder – *Currypulver*

B6 Indian food in Britain

a) Read the text. Try to guess the meaning of new words.

Many Indians live in Britain, so Indian food has become quite popular there. You can find Indian takeaways or restaurants in most towns. In Manchester people like to go to the famous 'Curry Mile': a long street with hundreds of Indian restaurants. You can eat all kinds of typical meals at such places, for example curries. The Indian curry is a dish with vegetables or meat in a special sauce. You have it with rice.
Restaurants also serve many other kinds of Indian food, such as biryani (a rice dish with meat), dhal (a lentil dish) and different kinds of bread, like naan and chapati. Traditionally, Indians use a lot of different spices. Some spices are really hot, like chillies. One very hot dish is curry vindaloo.
However, the dishes in Indian restaurants in Britain are often sweeter and milder than original Indian food. The most popular of them is chicken tikka masala. Some people say it has replaced fish and chips as the 'national dish of Britain'.

M model text

b) What information is new to you? Talk to a partner.

c) Write about food from another country that is popular in Germany (Turkish, Italian, Russian, Japanese, ...) in your exercise book.

Write at least four sentences.

Write at least six sentences. Include some information about typical dishes.

Write at least eight sentences. Include some information about:
- **typical dishes and the ingredients for them,**
- **the original food and the dishes in restaurants in Germany.**

B7 A crossword

Fill in the words.

Down ↓
1 Someone who behaves nicely and cares about other people's feelings is ...
2 a text that tells you what to do
3 a combination of different things
5 a deep round dish that you use for holding food, for example salad
7 a deep round container that you use for cooking food

Across →
4 There are lots of them on trees.
6 A person or a thing that many people like is ...
8 People use it to put sugar in their coffee or tea.

B8 Different ways of eating

☆ **Look at the texts and your notes from TB B9 again. Then match the countries to the information.**

1	In Britain	A	people usually eat soup after the main course.		1	
2	In Iran	B	people never cut spaghetti with a knife.		2	
3	In France	C	many people like chips and crisps with salt and vinegar.		3	
4	In China	D	people serve food on special trays.		4	
5	In India	E	snails are a speciality.		5	
6	In Italy	F	people pick up their food with pieces of chapati.		6	
7	In Japan	G	families often sit on the floor around a large cloth.		7	

☾ **Look at the texts and your notes from TB B9 again. Then read these statements. Write down which countries the people are from.**

1 *My mum and my grandma make fresh chapatis almost every day.*

2 *I started eating with chopsticks when I was four years old. My favourite food is sushi.*

3 *My mum bought a new cloth for our meals. It's really pretty. We put it on the floor and sit around it.*

4 *Yesterday I saw some tourists in a restaurant. They cut their spaghetti. I thought that was funny. We never do that.*

5 *We had a nice meal last night. My parents bought new chopsticks for all of us. First we had meat, vegetables and rice. After that we had soup.*

6 *We had guests from Germany last weekend. We showed them how to eat snails with a special holder and a small fork. They really liked them.*

7 *I like chips with ketchup, but like many people in my country I think that chips with salt and vinegar are simply the best.*

Speaker 1 is from ____________________.

Speaker 2 is from ____________________.

Speaker 3 is from ____________________.

Speaker 4 is from ____________________.

Speaker 5 is from ____________________.

Speaker 6 is from ____________________.

Speaker 7 is from ____________________.

☼ **Look at the texts and your notes from TB B9 again. Then answer these questions in your exercise book.**

1. In which countries don't people usually eat with knives and forks?
2. You go to a fish and chips shop in Britain. What can you put on the chips?
3. An Italian family invites you for a spaghetti dinner. What do you have to know?
4. Do you think the Japanese way of eating is comfortable? Give reasons.

5. If you invited a person from India, would you serve them a hamburger? Why or why not?
6. What do Chinese people do to show they are enjoying a meal?
7. Do you think it is easy or difficult to eat snails? Give reasons.
8. What would you ask people from Iran about their eating habits? Write down at least three questions.

B9 Choose

1. **Look at Theme 1B again. How many dishes or kinds of food can you find? Where do they come from? Make a list.**

country	dishes / kinds of food
Spain	paella
India	chicken curry ...
...	...

2. **Write the recipe for your favourite dish. Add pictures or photos.**

3. **Find a picture of a typical German meal or a typical meal from your parents' or grandparents' home country. What is it? How do you prepare it? When do people eat it? Present some interesting facts to the class.**

B10 Target task: A presentation about Greek food

a) **Listen to a presentation about Greek food. Number the photos in the right order.**

CD 16

model text

typical desserts: baklava and kataifi

typical starters: mezedes

a Greek family meal

koulouri

typical main courses: moussaka and souvlaki

b) **If you had to give the pupils feedback on their presentation, what would you tell them? Listen again and make notes. Then compare your ideas in class.**

Tipp
Hört euch die Präsentation noch einmal an, bevor ihr mit TB B11 anfangt.

Die *Test-yourself*-Seiten bieten dir die Möglichkeit zu überprüfen, was du gelernt hast. Du kannst frei entscheiden, ob du Aufgaben mit einem Stern, einem Mond oder einer Sonne bearbeiten möchtest. Natürlich kannst du auch „mischen", zum Beispiel Stern- und Mond-Aufgaben. Bearbeite die Aufgaben dann nacheinander. Schlage die Lösungen ab Seite 121 nach und berechne deine Punkte. Trage sie in die lilafarbenen Kästen am Rand ein. Lies dann die Erläuterungen zur Bewertung auf Seite 21. Sieh dir die bearbeiteten *Test-yourself*-Seiten noch einmal an, bevor du den Portfolio-Fragebogen zu *Theme 1* ausfüllst.

T1 Listening: Are you ready to order?

CD 23

☆ **a) Listen to two scenes. Where are the people? Tick the right restaurants.**

☐ an Italian place ☐ a curry house
☐ a Japanese restaurant ☐ a Chinese restaurant

b) Listen again. What do the people order? Tick the right answers.

Scene 1:

☐ chicken tikka masala ☐ chicken curry ☐ vegetable masala ☐ naan

Scene 2:

☐ spicy noodles ☐ sushi ☐ spicy fish soup ☐ spicy fish on crispy rice

von 12

CD 24

☾ **a) Listen to three scenes. Where are the people? Tick the right restaurants.**

☐ an Italian place ☐ a curry house ☐ a Japanese restaurant
☐ a pub ☐ a Chinese restaurant ☐ a fast food restaurant

b) Listen again. What do the people order? Tick the right answers.

Scene 1:

☐ chicken tikka masala ☐ chicken curry ☐ vegetable masala ☐ naan

Scene 2:

☐ spicy noodles ☐ sushi ☐ spicy fish soup ☐ spicy fish on crispy rice

Scene 3:

☐ fish and chips ☐ fish fingers ☐ cheeseburger ☐ small salad

von 18

CD 25

☼ **a) Listen to four scenes. Where are the people? Tick the right restaurants.**

☐ a curry house ☐ a fast food restaurant ☐ a Japanese restaurant
☐ a Chinese restaurant ☐ a pub ☐ an Italian place

b) Listen again. What do the people order? Take notes.

Scene 1: ____________________

Scene 2: ____________________

Scene 3: ____________________

Scene 4: ____________________

von 26

T2 Reading: Eating habits in Great Britain

Read about British people's eating habits.

Many traditional British dishes are made with meat, fish, potatoes, flour, butter and eggs. Sandwiches, fish and chips, roasts[1] and savoury pies are some very typical British foods. During the week many pupils and adults take a 'packed lunch' in a plastic box with them to school and to work. This is often a sandwich, a small bag of crisps, a piece of fruit and a drink. The evening meal is called 'tea', 'dinner' or 'supper'. For a long time, a typical dish for this meal was meat and 'two veg'. Usually one of the vegetables was potatoes. Today British people prefer to eat curry, pasta or rice dishes in the evening.
On Sundays many families still like to have a traditional meal for lunch: the Sunday Roast. It is a dish of roast meat (beef, lamb or pork) that you eat with gravy, vegetables, potatoes and Yorkshire pudding.
If British people invite you to their house for a meal, be very polite. Bring them a little present, for example flowers or chocolates. Always say "thank you" when they serve you something. Wait until everyone starts eating. Don't talk with food in your mouth.

[1] roast – *Braten*

☆ **Tick right or wrong.**

	right	wrong
1. British people often have sandwiches for lunch.	☐	☐
2. Supper is an afternoon meal.	☐	☐
3. 'Two veg' means 'two vegetarians'.	☐	☐
4. A roast is a meat dish.	☐	☐

von 8

☾ **Tick right or wrong.**

	right	wrong
1. Traditional British dishes are made with pasta and rice.	☐	☐
2. During the week many people take a 'packed breakfast' with them.	☐	☐
3. There are three different words for the evening meal in Britain.	☐	☐
4. A roast is always a pork dish.	☐	☐
5. If British people invite you for a meal, they will give you flowers.	☐	☐

von 10

☼ **Answer the questions.**

1. What is a 'packed lunch'? ______________________________
2. What is the evening meal called in Britain? ______________________________
3. What does 'two veg' mean? ______________________________
4. What is a Sunday Roast? ______________________________
____
5. What shouldn't you do if you eat at a British person's house? (two things) ______________
____

von 10

Tipp
Nehmt euren Dialog auf oder führt ihn in der Klasse vor.

T3 Speaking: Ordering food

☆ **Act out the dialogue.**

von 4

Partner/in A: Kellner/Kellnerin	Partner/in B: Gast
1 Begrüße B und frage, ob er/sie bestellen möchte.	2 Bejahe die Frage und sage, was du essen möchtest.
3 Frage B, was er/sie trinken möchte.	4 Antworte.

☾ **Act out parts 1–6.** ☼ **Act out the whole dialogue.**

von 6

von 12

Partner/in A: Kellner/Kellnerin	Partner/in B: Gast
1 Begrüße B und frage, ob er/sie bestellen möchte.	2 Sage, was du essen möchtest.
3 Frage B, ob er/sie irgendwelche Beilagen möchte.	4 Bejahe die Frage und sage, welche Beilage oder Beilagen du möchtest.
5 Frage B, was er/sie trinken möchte.	6 Antworte.
7 Serviere dann das Essen und sage „Bitte“.	8 Bedanke dich. Wenn du mit dem Essen fertig bist, frage, ob du die Rechnung haben kannst.
9 Antworte, dass du gleich bei B sein wirst. Nenne dann den Preis.	10 Bezahle.
11 Bedanke dich und wünsche B noch einen schönen Abend.	12 Bedanke dich und wünsche A ebenfalls einen schönen Abend.

T4 Writing: Your favourite food

Write about your favourite food. What is it? Where does it come from? How does it taste? Where do you eat it? Who cooks it for you? You can write about one or more dishes.

☆ **Write five sentences.** ☾ **Write eight sentences.** ☼ **Write ten sentences.**

von 10

von 16

von 20

T5 Mediation: At Pizza World

Read the menu. Then answer …

☆ **two questions. You can choose.**

☾ **three questions. You can choose.**

☼ **all the questions.**

1. Wie viel bezahlt man für die billigste und wie viel für die teuerste große Pizza?

____

____

2. Dein Freund mag keine Zwiebeln. Kann er die Pizza Via Veneto bestellen?

____

3. Gibt es auch vegetarische Pizza?

____

4. Gibt es etwas mit Fleisch, aber nicht mit Salami oder Schinken?

____

Pizza World

Pizzas	**regular**	**large**
Ciao Bambino (V) *(tomatoes, cheese)*	£5.95	£7.75
Via Veneto *(ham, olives, garlic)*	£7.95	£10.35
Mexicana (V) *(beans, chillies, olives, onions)*	£8.95	£11.65
Capri *(salami, mushrooms, onions)*	£9.45	£12.25
Verde (V) *(onions, broccoli, mushrooms)*	£9.95	£12.95

Fresh salads		**Drinks**	
Italian salad	£6.45	Soft drinks	£1.50
Tomato salad	£5.45	Water	£1.40
Chicken salad	£7.45	Coffee / tea	£1.45

5. Was musst du bezahlen, wenn du eine normale Pizza Capri, einen Tomatensalat und ein Wasser bestellst?

____

von 4

von 6

von 10

Trage die Punkte, die du erreicht hast, in diese Tabelle ein. Achte darauf, wie die Aufgabe gekennzeichnet ist (Stern, Mond oder Sonne). Insgesamt trägst du fünf Ergebnisse ein.

	☆	☾	☼
Listening	____ von 12	____ von 18	____ von 26
Reading	____ von 8	____ von 10	____ von 10
Speaking	____ von 4	____ von 6	____ von 12
Writing	____ von 10	____ von 16	____ von 20
Mediation	____ von 4	____ von 6	____ von 10

Mithilfe dieser Übersichten findest du heraus, wie du bei den einzelnen Aufgaben abgeschnitten hast. Markiere die Felder, die auf dich zutreffen.

	☆			☾			☼		
	Super!	Gut!	Nur Mut!	Super!	Gut!	Nur Mut!	Super!	Gut!	Nur Mut!
Listening	12–9	8–5	4–0	18–13	12–7	6–0	26–18	17–10	9–0
Reading	8–6	5–3	2–0	10–7	6–4	3–0	10–7	6–4	3–0
Speaking	4	3–2	1–0	6–5	4–3	2–0	12–9	8–5	4–0
Writing	10–7	6–4	3–0	16–12	11–6	5–0	20–14	13–8	7–0
Mediation	4	3–2	1–0	6–5	4–3	2–0	10–7	6–4	3–0

M1 Listening: A shopping list

CD 26

a) Listen to Karla and Gillian's plans for Saturday. What do they want to cook together?

- ☐ pasta with cream sauce and fruit sorbet
- ☐ pasta with tomato sauce and fruit salad
- ☐ pasta with garlic sauce and pineapple pie

b) Which is the girls' shopping list? Listen again and tick the right list.

Tipp
Du kannst dir beim Hören auf einem Blatt notieren, was die Mädchen kaufen wollen.

☐	☐	☐
tomatoes	pasta	pasta
olive oil	tomatoes	tomatoes
onion	onion	garlic
apple	carrot	carrot
banana	pineapple	pineapple
orange	banana	banana
lemon	orange	orange
mango	mango	lemon

M2 Reading: International food

Read what some children say about typical food in their countries. Then tick right or wrong.

In France, people love baguette. We eat it for breakfast with butter and jam. Normally we eat it with dinner, too.

Lunch in Spain is usually between 2 and 4 pm. It is a big meal and starts with salad or soup. Then we have a fish or a meat dish. For dessert we eat fruit, cake, or *flan*, which is made with milk, eggs and sugar.

For people in Russia, a typical fast breakfast is a sandwich with butter and cheese or sausage. Adults drink strong tea or coffee. When we have time, we cook eggs, porridge[1] or pancakes.

In Germany there are lots of different kinds of bread. For dinner, many people eat slices of bread with butter and cheese, ham or salami.

Mexican food is great. For breakfast I like thin, round breads called tortillas. They are filled with fried eggs and a sauce of chilli, tomato and onion.

Food is very important in Turkey. We have meat dishes, salad, yoghurt and many side dishes like olives for dinner. There is always freshly baked bread called *pide*. We eat lots of fruit, too.

[1] porridge – *Porridge, Haferbrei*

	right	wrong
1. There are more than three kinds of bread in Germany.	☐	☐
2. Tortillas are fried eggs with a special sauce.	☐	☐
3. Turkish people have a variety of fresh and cooked dishes for dinner.	☐	☐
4. French people eat baguette with butter and cheese for breakfast.	☐	☐
5. Russians always have eggs, porridge or pancakes in the morning.	☐	☐
6. Spanish people usually have a starter, a main course and dessert for lunch.	☐	☐

M3 Words: Verbs and nouns

Fill in the missing words.

verb	noun
choose	
	cook
mean	
	practice
mix	

verb	noun
start	
	holder
drink	
	invitation
present	

M4 Grammar: How much? How many?

Fill in 'much' or 'many'.

How ____________ butter have we got?

How ____________ people came to your party?

How ____________ gravy shall we make?

How ____________ spices should we buy?

How ____________ pineapples have you got?

How ____________ is the chicken wrap?

How ____________ are those Indian herbs?

How ____________ eggs are there in the fridge?

How ____________ curry paste do we need?

How ____________ bananas do you put in raita?

LiF p. 130
1

M5 Grammar: Food facts

Add the question tags.

aren't they • aren't you • can't you • doesn't it • don't you • don't they • hasn't it • haven't they • isn't it

1. You roll spaghetti around a fork, ____________________?
2. Paella is a traditional Spanish dish, ____________________?
3. People in Japan and China use chopsticks, ____________________?
4. The Japanese have got special trays for their food, ____________________?
5. Family meals are important for people in Iran, ____________________?
6. The English word 'pudding' means 'dessert', ____________________?
7. You can order bean burgers at the Food Express, ____________________?
8. The Safari Restaurant has got a lunchtime buffet bar, ____________________?
9. Steven, you're a vegan, ____________________?

LiF p. 131
3

D1 Who?

Find the answers in Theme 1.

1. Who eats Cornish Farmhouse Chicken? ____________________
2. Who can read Chinese? ____________________
3. Who makes spaghetti in a really big pot? ____________________
4. Who finds a fly in his soup? ____________________

D2 Give me five!

Look at Theme 1 again and find ...

- five starters: ____________________
- five main courses: ____________________
- five side dishes: ____________________
- five drinks: ____________________
- five adjectives to talk about food: ____________________

D3 A word quiz

How many words can you find in 'Yorkshire pudding'?

____

____

____

D4 A food limerick

Say the limerick. If you like, learn it by heart.

A vegetarian called Pam
Wouldn't eat pork or ham.
Well, to tell you the truth,
She had a sweet tooth
And all she would eat was jam.

A1 An interview

a) Unscramble the questions.

Questions	Answers
1. doing • you • What • in your free time • like • do • ?	
2. your favourite place • is • in your area • What • ?	
3. to do • would • What • you • next weekend • like • ?	

b) Now ask a partner the questions and take notes about his or her answers.

c) Tell the class about the person you have interviewed.

Mia likes meeting her friends.

Anton's favourite place is the zoo.

Luis would like to go to a skatepark next weekend.

...

A2 Things to do

a) Watch the video clip. What can the people do where they live? Take notes.

DVD 6

	what the people can do where they live
Eran	
Martin	
Fergus	
Rosa	
Jessica and Abigail	
Vicky and Ken	

b) Are there similar things you can do in your area? What other activities are possible in your area? Talk in class.

A3 Where to go

CD 1/12

a) Listen to TB A4. Where do the friends want to go? Why? Take notes.

	where he/she wants to go	reasons
Karla		
Rajiv		
Gillian		
David		

b) Read the questions. Then listen again and answer two questions. Take notes.

Read the questions. Then listen again and answer all the questions. Take notes.

1. Why doesn't Rajiv want to go to the Radio London Pop Concert?

____

2. Why doesn't Gillian want to do the Harry Potter walk?

____

3. Why doesn't David want to take part in the Beastly Run?

____

4. Why doesn't David want to go to Portobello Market?

____

A4 What is it?

a) Read the sentences and fill in the phrases.

classmates • flyer • decision • car boot sale • events • musical

LiF p. 131 4

1. A _______________ is a sale of things which come out of the back of a car.
2. A _______________ is a choice that you make after thinking carefully.
3. Your _______________ are the pupils who are in your class at school.
4. A _______________ is a piece of paper which informs you about events or products.
5. A _______________ is a theatre play with actors that sing, dance and act.
6. _______________ are important things that happen.

b) **Be a language detective. Mark 'who', 'which' and 'that' in the sentences in a). When do you use the words? Complete the rules.**

After people you use ______________________ or ______________________.

After things you use ______________________ or ______________________.

Complete these explanations. Use your own words.

1. A hero is a person ______________________________________.
2. Customers are people ______________________________________.
3. Trainers are shoes ______________________________________.
4. Computers are things ______________________________________.

A5 A special crossword

Read the definitions and fill in the words. Unscramble the other words.

Down ↓

1 Something that you buy at a really good price

2 A person who offers things, for example at a market or a car boot sale

5 A pretty thing that you wear on your ear

Across →

3 A place where you can see plays and musicals

4 A famous person's name, written by the the person himself or herself

6 If you are able to buy something, you can … it.

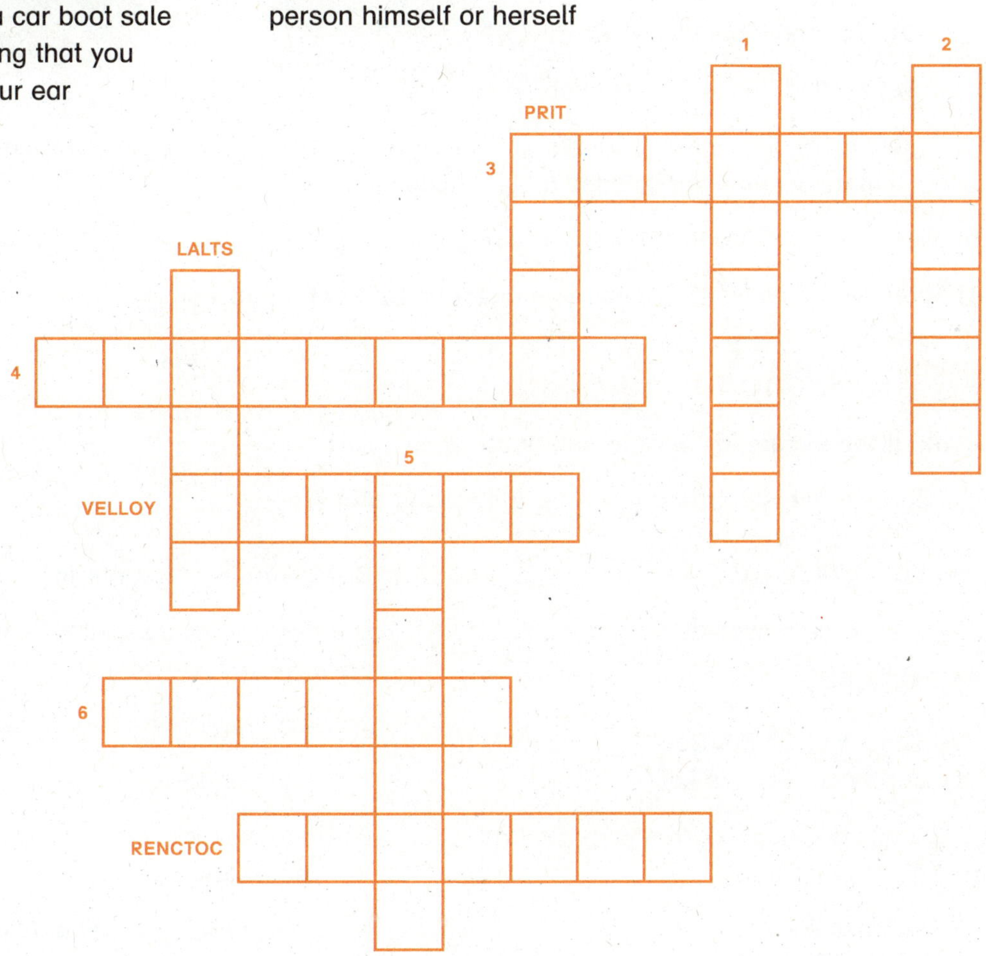

A6 Shopping dialogues

a) Read the dialogues and number them in the right order.

Dialogue 1

☐ **Layla:** Wow, they're really special. But too bad, I've only got £8.

☐ **Seller:** It's all right. I'll let you have one for £8.

☐ **Seller:** They're £9. I make them myself from old plastic bags.

☐ **Layla:** Oh, thank you very much. That's really kind of you. I'll take the purple and pink one then.

☐ **Layla's friend Sally:** I'll see how much I've got. Don't worry, I've got enough to help.

☐ **Layla:** I really like those bags. How much are they?

Dialogue 2

☐ **Owen:** Oh, great. That's a real bargain. I think my budgie will love it. Here's £10.

☐ **Owen:** Bye.

☐ **Seller:** You can have it for £6.

☐ **Owen:** I'm interested in the birdcage on the left in the car boot.

☐ **Owen:** I like it a lot. How much is it?

☐ **Seller:** And here's your change. Thank you very much. Bye.

☐ **Seller:** It's nice, isn't it? My daughter's first budgie lived in it for a while. Then she bought more budgies and needed a bigger cage.

CD 28 **b) Listen to the CD and check your dialogues.**

c) Work with a partner. Choose one dialogue and act it out.

A7 Looking for bargains

Look at the picture in TB A6 again. Work with a partner.

☆ **Choose one seller and make up a dialogue. Act it out.**

A Käufer/Käuferin

Überlege vorab, was du kaufen möchtest.

1 Begrüße B.

3 Sage, welche der Sachen dir gefällt, und frage, was sie kostet.

5 Sage, dass du die Ware nimmst, und gib B das Geld.

7 Verabschiede dich.

B Verkäufer/Verkäuferin

Überlege dir vorab englische Preise für deine Waren. Du kannst sie notieren.

2 Begrüße A.

4 Nenne den Preis.

6 Bedanke dich und gib A das Wechselgeld.

8 Verabschiede dich ebenfalls.

Choose one seller and make up a dialogue. Act it out.

A Käufer/Käuferin

Überlege vorab, was du kaufen möchtest. Suche zwei Dinge aus, die dir gefallen.

1 Begrüße B.

3 Sage, welche Waren dir gefallen, und frage, was die beiden Sachen kosten.

5 Sage, welche Ware du nimmst und warum du sie nimmst (gutes Produkt, guter Preis, ...). Gib B dann das Geld.

7 Verabschiede dich.

B Verkäufer/Verkäuferin

Überlege dir vorab englische Preise für deine Waren. Du kannst sie notieren.

2 Begrüße A.

4 Nenne die Preise und sage etwas zu den beiden Waren (z. B. dass sie fast neu sind, dass sie toll aussehen, dass du etwas selbst gemacht hast, ...).

6 Bedanke dich und gib A Wechselgeld.

8 Verabschiede dich ebenfalls.

Choose one seller and make up a dialogue. Act it out.

A Käufer/Käuferin

Überlege vorab, was du kaufen möchtest und für welchen Zweck du es haben willst (für dich selbst, als Geschenk, ...). Suche drei Dinge aus, die dir gefallen.

1 Begrüße B.

3 Sage, warum du etwas kaufen möchtest und welche Waren dir gefallen. Frage, was die einzelnen Sachen kosten.

5 Sage, wie viel Geld du dabei hast, und kommentiere die Preise (zu teuer, in Ordnung, ...). Sage dann, welche Ware du nimmst und begründe deine Entscheidung. Gib B das Geld.

7 Verabschiede dich.

B Verkäufer/Verkäuferin

Überlege dir vorab englische Preise für deine Waren. Du kannst sie notieren.

2 Begrüße A.

4 Nenne die Preise und sage etwas zu den Waren (z. B. dass sie fast neu sind, dass sie toll aussehen oder gut funktionieren, dass du etwas selbst gemacht hast, ...).

6 Bedanke dich und gib A Wechselgeld. Sage auch noch etwas zu der Auswahl (Beispiele: Wünsche A viel Freude mit der Ware oder dass sie gut ankommt, falls sie ein Geschenk ist).

8 Verabschiede dich ebenfalls.

A8 A word snake

a) Find the words from the story of 'The Lion King'.

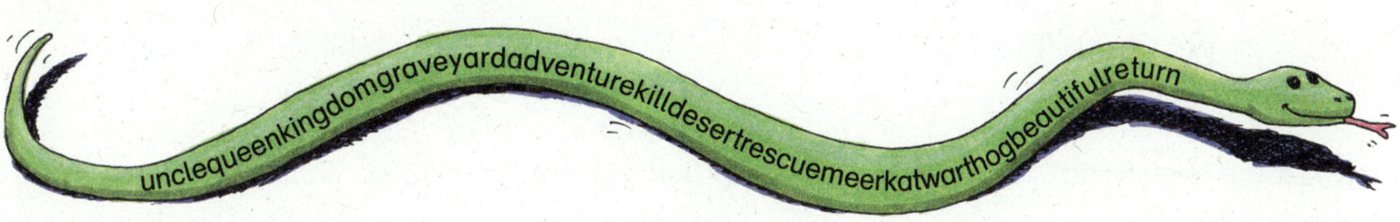

b) Write down the words. Then listen to the CD and check them.

CD 29

Write your own sentences with the words in your exercise book.

A9 The Lion King

☆ **Look at TB A9 again. Fill in the names of Simba's family and friends.**

1. ______________________ is Simba's father and ____________________ is his mother.
2. ________________________ is the lion king's brother and he is also Simba's uncle.
3. ____________________ is a young lioness. Later she and Simba fall in love.
4. Simba grows up with a meerkat, ______________, and a warthog, ______________.

☾ **Look at TB A9 again. Choose four questions and answer them in your exercise book.**

☼ **Look at TB A9 again and answer these questions in your exercise book.**

1. Why do you think Scar tells Simba about the Elephant Graveyard?
2. How does King Musafa die?
3. Why does Simba have to leave the kingdom?
4. How does he grow up after that?
5. What words and phrases describe Uncle Scar's character?
6. What is the 'Circle of Life'?

A10 Target task: A presentation about Christmas markets

a) Four German pupils have prepared a presentation about Christmas markets in Lüneburg. They give their classmates this list of new words. Look at the list.

town hall – *Rathaus*
accessory – *Accessoire*
booth – *Stand*
gingerbread – *Lebkuchen*
crystal lamp – *Kristalllampe*
fir – *Tanne*
wood – hier: *Wald*

hut – *Hütte*
inner courtyard – *Innenhof*
craftsman – *Handwerker*
trader – *Händler, Händlerin*
pottery – *Töpferwaren*
wrought iron work – *Kunstschmiedearbeit(en)*

CD 30

b) Now listen to the presentation and tick the details the pupils talk about.

- ☐ the lights
- ☐ the visitors from other places
- ☐ how long the markets last
- ☐ how you get to the markets
- ☐ the opening times
- ☐ Christmas concerts
- ☐ what adults and children can do
- ☐ what you can buy
- ☐ the shops in Lüneburg
- ☐ a historic market

c) Read the questions. Then listen again and tick the right answers.

1. What media and visuals[1] do the pupils use?

☐ some photos ☐ the board ☐ the whiteboard ☐ the Internet

2. What product do they present?

☐ a poster ☐ a recording ☐ a calendar ☐ a brochure

d) Do you think this is a good presentation? Say why or why not.

1 visuals – *Bildmaterial*

B1 A carnival blog

Who wrote this? Look at TB B5 again and write down the bloggers' names.

1. "I think Notting Hill Carnival is great!" That's ______
2. "It was my first carnival so I took a friend with me." ______
3. "I will go every year from now on!" ______
4. "Carnival? Not outside my front door!" ______
5. "I didn't like all the rubbish and the broken glass." ______
6. "I didn't just come for the carnival, but I'm glad I had the chance to go to it!" ______

Look at TB B5 again and tick the right names.

Who …	Tom	Kathy	Amet	Dan	Emma	Martyn	James
1. needs new bike tyres?	☐	☐	☐	☐	☐	☐	☐
2. enjoyed the steel bands?	☐	☐	☐	☐	☐	☐	☐
3. thinks the police did a good job?	☐	☐	☐	☐	☐	☐	☐
4. wants to go to the carnival every year from now on?	☐	☐	☐	☐	☐	☐	☐
5. saw a little girl who hurt herself on broken glass?	☐	☐	☐	☐	☐	☐	☐
6. went to the carnival with a friend?	☐	☐	☐	☐	☐	☐	☐

Tipp
Manchmal musst du zwei Namen markieren.

Look at TB B5 again and tick the right sentence endings.

1. Martin and James …
   - ☐ think the police have to put up more posters to tell people to be careful.
   - ☐ think the police did a good job with the many people at the carnival.
   - ☐ think the police had a few problems with the many people at the carnival.

2. Amet and Dan …
   - ☐ had a brilliant day and liked everything at the carnival.
   - ☐ didn't like a lot of things and so they didn't enjoy the carnival.
   - ☐ had a brilliant day although they also had negative experiences.

3. Emma …
   - ☐ lives in Notting Hill and hates the carnival because it makes life more difficult.
   - ☐ lives in Notting Hill and hates the carnival because she doesn't like steel bands.
   - ☐ likes the carnival, but not outside her front door.

4. Kathy …
   - ☐ was on holiday in London and therefore had the chance to go to the carnival.
   - ☐ came all the way from Australia just to see the carnival.
   - ☐ wants to go to Australia on holiday after the carnival.

B2 Do they like the carnival?

CD 34

a) Listen to a radio show in which four teenagers are talking about Notting Hill Carnival. Who likes the carnival and who doesn't? Tick the right answers.

how to listen TB p.143

	likes the carnival	doesn't like the carnival	reasons
Rufus			
Alice			
Leo			
Nadira			

b) Listen again. Why do the people like the carnival, or why don't they? Take notes under 'reasons'.

c) Compare your notes with a partner.

d) Use your notes to write about ...

two of the people **all of the people**

in your exercise book. Explain why they like or don't like Notting Hill Carnival.

B3 A great street party

Read the text. Then add adjectives. You can choose from the box or use your own ideas.

big • colourful • delicious • different • exciting • fantastic • fun • funny • good • great • interesting • little • long • nice • second-hand • small • tasty • wonderful • yummy • ...

model text

Tipp
Vor Vokalen verwendest du „an".

Each July we have a__ ____________ party in our street. It is ____________!

All our neighbours put up ____________ stalls. They sell ____________ food and drinks. My parents always make ____________ cakes and desserts. There are ____________ tables where you can sit down and eat. At some stalls you can also buy ____________ clothes and toys. There is a__ ____________ band that plays ____________ music. And there is a__ ____________ clown. She plays with the ____________ children, but it is also fun for the adults to watch her. When I was younger I didn't know who she was but now I know that it is Frau Berger, the ____________ woman who lives in number 29.

B4 Who or what is it?

a) Read the definitions and fill in 'who', 'which' or 'that'.

Definitions	Who or what is it?
1. It is a man __________ works for the police:	__________
2. It is the time of day __________ follows the evening:	__________
3. It is a group of people __________ play music:	__________
4. It is an instrument ________ you hit with your hands or with sticks:	__________
5. It is a person __________ steals things out of pockets or bags:	__________
6. It is a word __________ means the same as 'country':	__________
7. It is someone __________ comes to live in a new country:	__________
8. It is a set of clothes __________ you wear for carnival:	__________

LiF p. 131 4

Tipp
Du kannst die Wortliste auf Seite 209–213 im Textbook zu Hilfe nehmen.

b) Now write down who or what it is.

Write at least three more definitions into your exercise book. Your partner says who or what it is.

B5 Safety tips for the carnival

Work with a partner or in a small group. Read the safety tips. Then say in German what the tips are about.

Man sollte ...

Man kann ...

Es ist sinnvoll, ...

Am besten ...

NOTTING HILL CARNIVAL SAFETY TIPS

- Leave your car at home. Take the tube or bus instead. It is best to plan your journey in advance because some Tube stations are closed during Notting Hill Carnival.
- Don't put your wallet or mobile phone in the back pocket of your trousers.
- If you have any worries, inform a police officer – you are never far from one at the carnival.
- Don't stand too close to the floats.
- Stay away from extremely crowded streets.
- Finding people at the carnival is very difficult. Try to meet your friends in other parts of London and then go to Notting Hill together.
- Stay together with your friends or family all the time.
- Wear comfortable shoes such as trainers.
- Drink lots of water, especially if the weather is hot.

how to mediate TB p. 145

B6 A colourful festival

Fill in 'who', 'which' or 'that'.

1. Notting Hill Carnival is a festival _______________ takes place every year in August.

LiF p. 131
4

2. Lots of visitors watch the parades _______________ move through the streets.
3. You can see lots of dancers _______________ wear fantastic costumes.
4. You can listen to bands _______________ play cool music.
5. There are food stalls _______________ serve delicious Caribbean food.

Make sentences.

Rajiv and his friends liked watching the people They sold samosas They sold the food at a stall They had lots of customers They gave the profits to an animal shelter	who which that	really liked their food. was outside the Patels' shop. were at the carnival. is in Notting Hill. were only 2 pounds.

____

____

____

____

____

Make one sentence from two. Use 'who', 'which' or 'that'.

1. Rajiv always loves watching the crowds of people. The people take part in the carnival.

____

2. This year he had a samosa stall. The samosa stall was outside his parents' shop.

____

3. Next to the stall there was a sign. The sign said, "Best samosas in Notting Hill here!"

____

4. Rajiv had lots of customers. The customers really liked his delicious food.

____

5. Rajiv didn't have time to talk to some classmates. Some classmates stopped at his stall.

____

B7 At the parade

What is happening in the pictures? Write at least three sentences about each picture.

cheer • dance • move • smile • stand • take photos • walk • watch • wave • wear • …

There are two ____________________

They are wearing ____________________

A boy ____________________

LiF p. 131 5R

B8 Your article

Complete this article in a German newspaper about the incident with the little boy at the carnival. You can look at TB B10c) for help.

how to mediate TB p. 145

Seite 12 | **Aus aller Welt** | Montag, 31. August

____________________ **beinahe von Festwagen überrollt**

Beim beliebten karibischen Karneval im Londoner Stadtteil Notting Hill ist der ____________________ ____________________.

Ein Taschendieb ____________________ ____________________, während sich das Kind mit seiner Mutter eine Parade ansah. Geistesgegenwärtig konnte ihn ein junger Trommler aus einer Steelband ____________________.

Die Mutter ____________________.

Die Polizei ____________________.

B9 Sound check

CD 36

a) Listen to the words and repeat them.

b) Sort the words into the lists. Watch out: one word does not fit into either list. Which word is it?

____

CD 37

c) Listen to the CD and check your lists.

throw • control • pocket • broken • profit • nothing • along • costume • local

/əʊ/	/ɒ/

B10 A cool concert

There was a concert on Talbot Street last night. Write down what the people were doing.

cry loudly • dance wildly • film the event • flirt with Vanessa • listen to the music • have some delicious food • play some really cool songs • watch a pickpocket

1. The DJ was playing ______________________________
2. A lot of people ______________________________

LiF p. 132 6

3. Gillian and Vanessa ______________________________
4. David ______________________________
5. The boy with the hat ______________________________
6. The policeman ______________________________
7. A little boy who wanted to go home ______________________________
8. A TV team ______________________________

B11 At Notting Hill police station

a) There are quite a few pickpockets at Notting Hill Carnival. Listen to two people and complete what they told the police.

Woman: While I ______________________________

a pickpocket ______________________________

Man: ______________________________ with a friend, ______

someone ______________________________

CD 38

b) Look at the pictures and write down what happened to three other people.

Roxana: have a soft drink – pickpocket: take her wallet

While Roxana ______________________________

____

LiF p. 132 6

Mr Fynn: listen to a steel band – girl: steal his camera

____

when ______________________________

Jenna: talk to her friend Rosy – pickpocket: push her

____

____

B12 Choose

Look at TB B10 and B11 again.

1. How would you describe the pickpocket? What does he look like? How old is he? What was he wearing at the parade? Write down what you would tell the police.
2. One of you steps into the role of the pickpocket and sits on a 'hot seat'. Some others ask him questions.
   If you play the pickpocket, think about what kind of person he is. Imagine what his life is like. Try to act like him.
   The others prepare questions they want to ask the pickpocket, for example about his family, his job, his reasons for stealing money, ...
3. A radio reporter talks to some visitors of the carnival who saw what happened to the little boy. Make up some dialogues and record them.

Auf Seite 21 kannst du noch einmal nachlesen, wie du mit den *Test-yourself*-Seiten arbeitest. Die Lösungen findest du ab Seite 122.

T1 Listening: Being a lion kid

CD 42

Tipp
Du kannst das Interview zweimal anhören.

☆ **Read the questions and answers. Then listen to a radio interview and tick the correct answers.**

1. How old is Nathan?	☐ 10	☐ 11	☐ 12
2. What is Nathan's role in 'The Lion King'?	☐ Timon	☐ Pumba	☐ young Simba
3. How long did he go to the Lion King Cub[1] School?	☐ 14 months	☐ 14 weeks	☐ 40 days
4. How often is he on stage?	☐ every day	☐ at the weekend	☐ twice a week

___ von 8

CD 42

☾ **Read the questions. Then listen to a radio interview and write down the answers.**

1. How old is Nathan? ______________________
2. What is Nathan's role in 'The Lion King'? ______________________
3. Who took him to a theatre school for kids? ______________________
4. How long did he go to the Lion King Cub[1] School? ______________________
5. How much did his parents have to pay for the school? ______________________
6. How often does Nathan perform now? ______________________

___ von 12

CD 42

☼ **Read the questions. Then listen to a radio interview and write down the answers.**

1. What is Nathan's role in 'The Lion King'? ______________________
2. Where did he take acting, singing and gymnastics lessons when he was younger?
____
3. What is the Lion King Cub[1] School? ______________________
____
4. How long did Nathan go to the Lion King Cub School? ______________________
5. Why does he like his role? Write down two reasons. ______________________
____
6. How often does Nathan perform now? ______________________

___ von 14

[1] cub – *Junges (von einem Tier)*

T2 Reading: A success story

Read about the musical 'The Lion King'.

The musical 'The Lion King' is based on the popular animated film[1] of the same name, which came out in 1994. It has got all the wonderful songs from the film, like 'The Circle of Life' and 'Hakuna Matata'. Many of the actors wear animal costumes. Some use special devices[2]. For example, those who play the giraffes walk on stilts[3].
The first performance of the musical took place in Minneapolis (USA), on 31 July 1997. Since then 'The Lion King' has been one of the most successful musicals ever. There have been productions in many places all over the world, such as New York, Toronto, London, Paris, Sydney, and Tokyo. Since December 2001 there have been performances at one of the theatres at the harbour in Hamburg. A large lion's head is used to decorate the entrance to the theatre, which is a huge place with 2030 seats. There are eight performances every week, so over the years millions of visitors have seen the musical. In January 2014, the 5000th performance took place. You can get to the theatre by car, bus or boat. Some boats are named after characters in the musical.

[1] animated film – *Zeichentrickfilm;* [2] device – *Gerät, Vorrichtung;* [3] stilt – *Stelze*

☆ **Match the sentence parts.**

1	The film 'The Lion King' came out	A	in 2001.	A	
2	The first performance of the musical 'The Lion King' was	B	in 1994.	B	
3	People could see the musical in Hamburg for the first time	C	in 2014.	C	
4	The 5000th performance in Hamburg took place	D	in 1997.	D	

von 8

☾ **Tick right or wrong.**

	right	wrong
1. In the musical 'The Lion King' you can see real animals on stage.	☐	☐
2. The first performance of the musical was in 1994.	☐	☐
3. There have been performances in Hamburg since 2001.	☐	☐
4. In January 2014, 5000 people came to see 'The Lion King' in Hamburg.	☐	☐
5. The theatre in Hamburg is big enough for 2030 people.	☐	☐

von 10

☼ **Complete the sentences.**

1. The first performance of the musical 'The Lion King' took place ________________ years after the animated film came out.
2. This performance took place in the American city ________________________________.
3. The actors who play the giraffes use ______________ as devices to move their costumes.
4. In Europe, there have been performances in __________ and ___________, for example.
5. The theatre in Hamburg is big enough for ______________ people.
6. There are around ______________ performances per month in Hamburg.

von 12

Tipp
Nehmt euren Dialog auf oder führt ihn in der Klasse vor.

T3 Speaking: Buying trainers

Work with a partner. Make notes for a shopping dialogue and then act it out.

☆ **Partner A (seller)**

1 Ask if you can help B.
3 Show B a pair of black trainers.
5 Say that they are £18.
7 Say thank you and goodbye.

Partner B (customer)

2 Say that you are looking for trainers.
4 Try the shoes on and ask for the price.
6 Say that you will take them and pay.
8 Also say goodbye.

von 8

☾ **Partner A (seller)**

1 Say hello and ask if you can help B.
3 Ask what size B needs.
5 Show B a pair of black trainers.
7 Say that they are £18.
9 Say thank you and goodbye.

Partner B (customer)

2 Say that you are looking for trainers.
4 Tell A what shoe size you need.
6 Try them on and ask for the price.
8 Say that it is a bargain and pay.
10 Also say goodbye.

von 10

☼ **Partner A (seller)**

1 Say hello and ask if you can help B.
3 Ask what size B needs.
5 Show B a pair of black trainers and say what is special about them.
7 Say that they are £18.
9 Give B the change. Then say thank you and goodbye.

Partner B (customer)

2 Say that you are looking for trainers.
4 Tell A what shoe size you need.
6 Try the trainers on and say why you like them. Then ask for the price.
8 Say something positive about the price and give B £20.
10 Also say goodbye.

von 10

T4 Writing: Events in your area

Write about a special event in your area. What is it? Where and when does it take place? What do you do there? How often do you go there? Why do you like it?

☆ **Write five sentences.** ☾ **Write eight sentences.** ☼ **Write ten sentences.**

Tipp
Schlage unbekannte Wörter nach.

von 10

von 16

von 20

T5 Mediation: A car boot sale

Read the poster and answer ... ☆ four questions. ☾ five questions. ☼ all the questions.

1. Wo findet der Kofferraum-Flohmarkt statt?

___

2. Wann findet er statt?

___

3. Wann beginnt und endet der Verkauf?

___

4. Was kostet der Eintritt?

___

5. Was kann man zu essen kaufen?

___

6. Was bedeuten die Preise für Autos?

___

7. Was muss man machen, wenn man weitere Informationen benötigt?

___

CAR BOOT SALE

Saturday, 29 August

Car pitches:	£ 7 prebooked £ 10 on the day
Entry:	Free to the public
Location:	Car park, Holloway Road
Stall set-up:	From 7:30 am
Sale open:	From 9 am to 4 pm

There will be drink stalls.

To ask for further details please call 01946 59147 or email wilma@burton.uk

___ von 8

___ von 10

___ von 14

Trage die Punkte, die du erreicht hast, in diese Tabelle ein. Achte darauf, wie die Aufgabe gekennzeichnet ist (Stern, Mond oder Sonne). Es sind insgesamt fünf Ergebnisse.

	☆	☾	☼
Listening	___ von 8	___ von 12	___ von 14
Reading	___ von 8	___ von 10	___ von 12
Speaking	___ von 8	___ von 10	___ von 10
Writing	___ von 10	___ von 16	___ von 20
Mediation	___ von 8	___ von 10	___ von 14

Finde nun heraus, wie du abgeschnitten hast. Markiere die Felder, die auf dich zutreffen.

	☆			☾			☼		
	Super!	Gut!	Nur Mut!	Super!	Gut!	Nur Mut!	Super!	Gut!	Nur Mut!
Listening	8–6	5–3	2–0	12–9	8–5	4–0	14–11	10–6	5–0
Reading	8–6	5–3	2–0	10–7	6–4	3–0	12–9	8–5	4–0
Speaking	8–6	5–3	2–0	10–7	6–4	3–0	10–7	6–4	3–0
Writing	10–7	6–4	3–0	16–12	11–6	5–0	20–14	13–8	7–0
Mediation	8–6	5–3	2–0	10–7	6–4	3–0	14–11	10–6	5–0

M1 Listening: A great car boot sale

CD 43

a) Listen to three dialogues at a car boot sale. Tick what the people buy.

1. In dialogue 1 a girl buys …

   ☐ a doll. ☐ a toy gorilla. ☐ some books.

2. In dialogue 2 a man and his son buy …

   ☐ three books about Caribbean food. ☐ three comics. ☐ a book with Spanish recipes.

3. In dialogue 3 a boy called Rohan buys …

   ☐ boots. ☐ running shoes. ☐ running shorts.

b) Listen again. How much do the people pay for the things? Write down the prices.

1. The girl pays £____________________. 2. The father pays £____________________.

3. Rohan pays £____________________.

M2 Reading: Carnival here and there

a) Here are two texts in one. Unscramble them and mark them in two different colours.

The festival is also famous for the delicious Caribbean food you can buy there.

In some cities there are big parades and parties.

Every year in winter a lot of Germans celebrate carnival.

At that time it was a small street party but today it is one of the biggest festivals in Europe.

Notting Hill Carnival started in 1959.

The celebrations usually take place seven weeks before Easter.

They often call it the 'fifth season'.

You can see many dancers, singers and steel bands on floats.

People wear costumes, dance and sing, sometimes even at work or at school.

About 1.5 million visitors come to see it every year in August.

b) Write the texts into your exercise book. Find a good order for the sentences.

M3 Grammar: Two fantastic days in Notting Hill

Write about Notting Hill Carnival.

Tipp
Hier gibt es viele Möglichkeiten. Versuche, Sätze zu bilden, die Sinn machen.

Notting Hill Carnival is an event The carnival is a great festival for people There are visitors There are some performances Calypso is one of the music styles DJ Norman is one of the people There are lots of food stalls	who which that	come to London just for the carnival. give performances every year. are interesting for children, too. serve all kinds of Caribbean food. is worth going to. come from the Caribbean. love Caribbean music.

____

____ LiF p. 131 4

____

____

____

____

M4 Grammar: A busy morning

On the first morning of the carnival the Patels were very busy in their shop. What was everyone doing? Fill in the right verb forms.

sort • fill • write • eat • carry

1. Mr Patel ______________________ the fridge in the shop with soft drinks. LiF p. 132 6
2. Mrs Patel ______________________ fresh fruit into different baskets.
3. Rajiv ______________________ food to his stall in front of the shop.
4. Sheree ______________________ a sign for Rajiv's stall.
5. Ruby ______________________ a banana.

M5 Grammar: Dangerous situations at the carnival

Complete the sentences with the verb forms.

were watching • was enjoying • were waiting • was laughing

grabbed • ran • took • noticed • tried

1. Justine ______________________ about some funny dancers when a boy ______________________ away her mobile. LiF p. 132 6
2. Someone ______________________ to steal Mr Jameson's sunglasses while he ______________________ some spicy Caribbean chicken at a food stall.
3. Two pickpockets ______________________ some tourists when they ______________________ a policeman and ______________________ away.
4. A man ______________________ Mrs Parker's bag while she and her husband ______________________ for the bus.

D1 Where?

Find the answers in Theme 2.

Where can you see …

1. a box with tennis balls? ____________
2. a woman with sunglasses? ____________
3. a map of the West Indies? ____________
4. a red guitar? ____________
5. a blue car? ____________
6. a child in a yellow costume? ____________

D2 Tongue twisters

Say these sentences as quickly as possible.

Sheree's brother is selling spicy samosas in the street.

Peter Pritchett picks pockets and purses.

Daisy Dickins dresses up and dances with Dave Donalds.

D3 Three, four, five, six

Look at Theme 2 and find …

- three words for valuable items: ____________
- four words for animals: ____________
- five things you can do at Notting Hill Carnival: ____________

  ____
- six things that you can buy at a car boot sale: ____________

  ____

D4 Strange tips

What's wrong with these tips for the carnival? Correct them.

1. Bring a lot of money with you so you can buy nice things.

   ____
2. Wear high heels[1] so you look pretty.

   ____
3. Stand near the floats so you can see the parade really well.

   ____

[1] high heels – *hochhackige Schuhe, Stöckelschuhe*

A1 Fitness instructions

a) Listen to the fitness instructions and read along. Then match them with the pictures.

CD 44

Exercise 1: Stand on your right leg. Take your left foot in both hands and pull[1] it to your back. Then stand on your left leg and pull your right foot.

Exercise 2: Stand in front of a chair. Hold your arms out in front of you. Sit down slowly. When you touch the chair, stand up again. Do this eight times.

Exercise 3: Sit on the floor. Bend forward[2] and hold your feet with your hands. Count to ten.

Exercise 4: Sit against a wall. Press[3] your back against it. Count to ten.

Exercise 5: Sit on the floor and bend your knees. Then move your upper body[4] back a little and lift your legs. Hold your arms out in front of you. Do this for 15 seconds.

Exercise 6: Stand on your left leg and put your right foot against your left knee. Put your hands on your head. Then stand on your right leg and put your left foot against your right knee.

[1] pull – *ziehen;* [2] bend forward – *sich vorwärts beugen;* [3] press – *drücken;* [4] upper body – *Oberkörper*

b) Choose three exercises. Listen to them again and do them.

c) Talk about the exercises in a group. Say ...
- **which exercises you did,**
- **if you found them easy or difficult,**
- **how long or how often you did them.**

I did exercise number 2. It was really easy for me. I did it eight times.

I tried to do exercise 5, but it was too difficult for me.

Think of another exercise and make notes. Then tell your classmates what to do.

A2 Can you do it?

a) Answer the questions.

Yes, I can. | No, I'm not. | Yes, I do. | ...

1. Can you do ten press-ups without stopping? ____________________
2. Are you out of breath when you run up stairs? ____________________
3. Do you do fitness exercises at home? ____________________
4. Have you got strong arms? ____________________
5. Can you run two kilometres? ____________________
6. Have you got skates? ____________________
7. Do you do sport for more than three hours a week? ____________________

b) Work with a partner. He or she has to answer the questions as quickly as possible. Then it is your turn to answer them. Close your workbooks when answering.

A3 A fitness fanatic and a couch potato

a) Write about the habits of these young women. Use the phrases in the box.

only like sports on TV • often go to the gym • go jogging at the weekend • often lie on the sofa • eat lots of crisps and sweets • do exercises in the morning • usually go to other places by car • walk a lot • not spend much time outside • eat lots of fruit and vegetables

The fitness fanatic ____________________

____

____

____

____

The couch potato ____________________

____

____

____

____

b) **How could the couch potato become fitter? Write down at least three tips. You can look at TB A2 and A4 for ideas.**

She could ______________________________

____

____

____

____

____

____

c) **Compare your ideas with a partner.**

Imagine a fitness fanatic and a couch potato meet at a party. Make notes for a dialogue. Act it out in class.

A4 Do you like or hate it?

a) **Listen to Gillian talking about sports. What does she like? What doesn't she like? Fill in the words.**

CD 45

Gillian likes ______________. She doesn't like ______________ some of the exercises before they start ______________. For example, she hates ______________ press-ups. But she thinks that ______________ up and down and ______________ on one foot are OK. Most of all she loves ______________.

LiF p. 132 7

b) **When doing sports, what do you like? What don't you like? Fill in the gaps.**

Tipp
Schlage neue Wörter nach.

I like ______________________________.

I'm really good at ______________________________.

I enjoy ______________________________.

I love ______________________________.

But I don't like ______________________________.

And I don't enjoy ______________________________.

I'm not good at ______________________________.

And I hate ______________________________.

A5 Do, go or play?

a) Sort the sports into the lists.

tennis • swimming • press-ups • skating • basketball • aerobics • running • volleyball • badminton • skiing • rope-skipping • dancing • ballet • hockey • karate

do	go	play

CD 46

b) Listen to the CD and check your lists.

c) Add one sport to each list.

Add two or three sports to each list.

A6 Nina's sport

CD 47

a) Listen to the CD. What is Nina's sport?

English Dancing ☐ Irish Dancing ☐ Ice Dancing ☐

b) Listen again and take notes.

when Nina started doing her sport: ______________________

why she started doing it: ______________________

____

what is special about the sport: ______________________

____

____

how often Nina goes to training: ______________________

special events: ______________________

what she needs for her sport: ______________________

____

what she doesn't like about it: ______________________

c) Compare your notes with a partner.

A7 Taller, fitter, faster

Look at these sports people and write at least five comparisons about them. Choose phrases from the box.

be fit • be slow • be successful • be athletic • be tall • be fast • be short

Logan is faster than Jacob. ________________

LiF p. 133 8R

A8 Choose

1. **Work in a group. Think of comparisons between different sports, sports people, teams or sports events. Write the sentence parts on big pieces of paper. Then give the pieces of paper to the people in your group. They must sort them and then read out the sentences.**

   Bayern München | is | more successful | than | Hannover 96.

2. **Choose at least twelve adjectives, for example from TB A7. Make a list like this for a partner. He or she has to complete it.**

fast		
	more popular	
		most athletic
...		

LiF p. 133 8R

3. **Work in a group. Sit in a circle. You need a soft ball. The person who starts says an adjective and throws the ball to another person. Person 2 has to say the comparative. Then he or she throws the ball to the next person who says the superlative and a new adjective. Play ten or more rounds.**

Successful!

More successful!

Most successful! – Strong!

A9 Becoming a winner

how to work with a dictionary TB p. 149

a) Read the portrait of Andy Murray. Look up new words.

Andrew (Andy) Murray is a professional tennis player and member of the British Davis Cup team. He was born in Glasgow, Scotland, on 15 May, 1987. Andy, who is 1.90 m tall, plays a two-handed backhand.
He started playing tennis at the age of three and won his first important title, the Orange Bowl, in Florida at the age of twelve. When he was 15, he decided to become a professional tennis player. He moved to Barcelona for 18 months where he trained with very good coaches.
Andy has had an amazing career. He has taken part in a large number of tournaments all over the world and was the winner of the 2012 Olympic Games, the 2012 US Open as well as the 2013 and 2016 Wimbledon Championships. He has also won titles in many other important tennis finals. He is one of the most successful British tennis players ever.
Together with football star David Beckham, Andy helped start the charity *Malaria No More UK*. He has also taken part in several charity tennis events.

b) Fill in words from the text.

1. When you play a sport as a job, you are a ______________________ player.
2. A ______________________ is someone who trains sports people.
3. A ______________________ is a sports competition with different games.
4. You win a ______________ when you beat everyone else in a sports competition.

c) Complete the fact file about Andy Murray.

Name:	**Country:**
Age:	**Sport:**
Career:	
Other interesting facts:	

d) Find out more interesting facts.
Add ... ☆ one fact ☾ two facts ☼ three facts to the fact file.

how to talk TB p. 143

e) Use your fact file to give a short talk about Andy Murray. Record it.

f) Work in a group. Listen to your recordings and give each other feedback.

A10 Lots of fundraising ideas

a) Look at TB A9 again and answer the questions.

1. Who has to think of fundraising ideas for school?

____

2. What are they raising money for, and why?

____

b) What are the children's ideas? How do they explain what the pupils could do?

☆ **Write three of their ideas into the list. Take notes.**

☾ **Write all their ideas into the list. Take notes.**

☼ **Write all their ideas into the list. Take notes. Then find out more about the ideas that Gillian, Charlie and David don't explain in detail.**

how to read TB p. 144

fundraising idea	details about the idea	your rating[1]
read-a-thon		

[1] rating – *Einschätzung, Einstufung*

c) Compare your lists in class.

d) Which ideas do you like? Which don't you like? Add your rating.

very good: 3 good: 2 OK: 1 not very good : 0

e) Talk about your ratings. Then have a vote. What are the three top fundraising ideas?

I think a ... is the best fundraising idea because ...

Well, I think a ... is really good, too.

B1 Charlie at the doctor's

a) Look at TB B1a) again. Tick the sentences you can find in the dialogue.

1. "My finger hurts a little." ☐
2. "Oh Charlie, don't make such a fuss!" ☐
3. "We'll be playing basketball again soon." ☐
4. "I wonder how much money we raised …" ☐
5. "The doctor will see you now." ☐
6. "Come on, Charlie. David, you wait here." ☐
7. "I think I've broken my hand." ☐
8. "The X-ray room is the second door on the right." ☐

b) Talk to a partner.

Sentence number … is in the dialogue. It's … who says it.

Sentence number … is not in the dialogue.

a) Look at TB B1a) again. Then close your book and tick right or wrong.

	right	wrong
1. Charlie's arm hurts and it is swollen.	☐	☐
2. Charlie is in the waiting room with David and David's father.	☐	☐
3. David kicked Charlie's finger during a football match.	☐	☐
4. The teachers won the football match against the pupils.	☐	☐
5. Charlie fell during the football match.	☐	☐
6. The doctor wants to take an X-ray.	☐	☐
7. The receptionist tells Charlie where the X-ray room is.	☐	☐

b) Correct the wrong sentences in your exercise book.

a) Look at TB B1a) again. Then close your book and tick right or wrong.

	right	wrong
1. Charlie hurt his finger because he fell when he was playing football.	☐	☐
2. The teacher thinks that Charlie is making a fuss.	☐	☐
3. David kicked Charlie's finger during a football match.	☐	☐
4. Charlie has to wait for one and a half hours until he can see the doctor.	☐	☐
5. David goes into the doctor's office with Charlie.	☐	☐
6. The pupils won the football match against the teachers.	☐	☐
7. Charlie says that they raised a lot of money.	☐	☐
8. The receptionist tells Charlie where the X-ray room is.	☐	☐

b) Correct the wrong sentences in your exercise book.

B2 What's wrong with them?

a) Look at the pictures and write about the people's health problems.

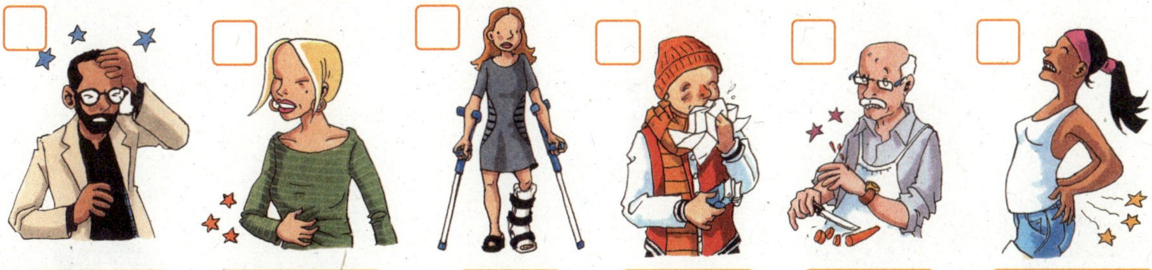

Mr Burns | Ms Hoover | Kylie | Victoria | Mr Tyler | Ms O'Neill

Mr Burns has

wordbank health TB p. 160

b) Listen to the six people. Who speaks first, second, ...? Number the pictures.

CD 58

B3 What happened?

a) Look at these scenes. Write down what the people were doing and what happened.

Chloe: play hockey – hurt her foot

Mrs Holmes: try to catch the bus – fall and bruise her knee

Mr Quinn: watch a fast sports car – walk into a door

LiF p. 132 6

Jacob: skateboard – roll into a hole and break his leg

Sadie: meet her friend in the park – suddenly feel ill

Aidan: do karate – hurt his shoulder

Chloe was playing hockey when she hurt her foot.

Mrs Holmes

b) Listen to the CD and check your sentences.

CD 59

B4 Life can be dangerous

a) Write down what has happened to the people.

LiF p. 130
2R

Oliver has eaten ____________________

Alyssa ____________________

Mr Clark ____________________

Ms Thompson ____________________

Savannah ____________________

Jordan ____________________

b) Look at the pictures again. What aren't the people able to do?

isn't able to • can't

ride his bike at the moment • cook for her family • eat cake at his friend's birthday party • play the guitar • go ice skating again tomorrow • write emails

LiF p. 133
9R

____

____

____

____

____

____

c) Work with a partner. Choose one of the people and make up a scene. The person tells a family member (parent, brother, wife, ...) or a friend ...

- **what has happened to him or her,**
- **how he or she feels.**

The family member or friend gives the person some good advice. Act out your scene.

B5 Dana's health problem

a) Complete the text about Dana's health problem.

can • can't • is able to • isn't able to • will be able to • has to • doesn't have to

LiF p. 133 9R

Dana doesn't feel well today. She has stomach ache and ________________ go to school. She thinks she ate too much pizza at her friend's party yesterday. She ______________ stay in bed all day and drink lots of tea. Dana ________________ eat anything except vegetable soup and dry bread, but luckily she ______________________________ take any medicine. Of course, she _______________ meet her friends, but she _____________ send them text messages. She _______________ also listen to music and read. If she is better by tomorrow, she _____________________________ get up at 7 o'clock and go back to school.

Tipp
Es gibt manchmal verschiedene Möglichkeiten.

b) What can people with different health problems do? What can't they do? Note down your ideas.

A person with ...	isn't able to	has to	can	doesn't have to
toothache				
earache				
a broken arm				
a temperature				
a bruised leg				

c) Talk about your notes in class.

B6 Sound check

a) Listen to the CD and repeat the words.

CD 60

/bru:z/	/'swəʊlən/	/'hedeɪk/	/'medsn/
______________	______________	______________	______________
/'bændɪdʒ/	/'tu:θeɪk/	/'hɒspɪtl/	/'temprɪtʃə/
______________	______________	______________	______________

b) Write down the words.

c) Look at the word list on pages 221–223 in your textbook and check your spelling.

B7 If ...

can • can't • will be able to • have to • will

a) Complete the sentences.

1. If you think you've broken your leg, you ______________________________ see a doctor.
2. If the doctor takes an X-ray, he or she ______________ see exactly what the problem is.
3. If your leg is broken, you ______________________________ need a cast[1].
4. If you have a cast, you ______________________________ do sport for some time.
5. If you are careful, you ______________________________ walk again after a few weeks.

[1] cast – *Gips*

b) Compare your sentences with a partner.

LiF p. 134
10

a) Write about a health problem.

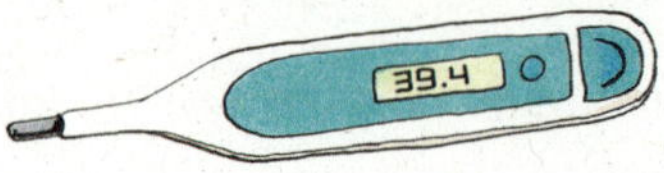

1. have a temperature – have to stay in bed

If you ______________________________

2. also have a headache – can take some medicine

____

3. not be hungry – not have to eat anything

____

4. not be able to read – can listen to music

____

5. sleep a lot – will soon feel better

____

CD
61

b) Listen to the CD and check your sentences.

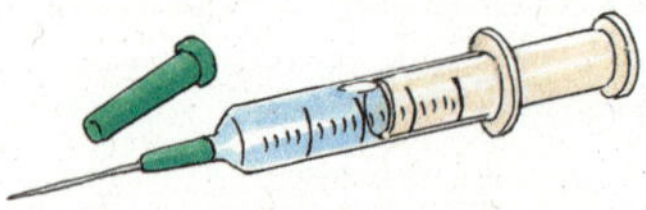

a) Complete the sentences. Use your own ideas.

1. If you have chickenpox, ______________________________
2. You will need an injection if you ______________________________
3. If you hurt both your hands, ______________________________
4. You will have to stay at home if you ______________________________
5. If you have a tooth pulled out, ______________________________
6. You can't eat too much fat or sugar if you ______________________________

b) Compare your sentences with a partner.

B8 How to help out at the doctor's

Niko from Gelsenkirchen and his friend Louise from England went on a bike ride. Louise fell and hurt her leg. Now they are at the doctor's. Louise doesn't speak German. How can Niko help out? Write down what he says.

Empfangsdame: Dr. Schüssler wird dich in einigen Minuten untersuchen.
Louise: What did she say?

Niko: ______________________________

how to mediate TB p. 145

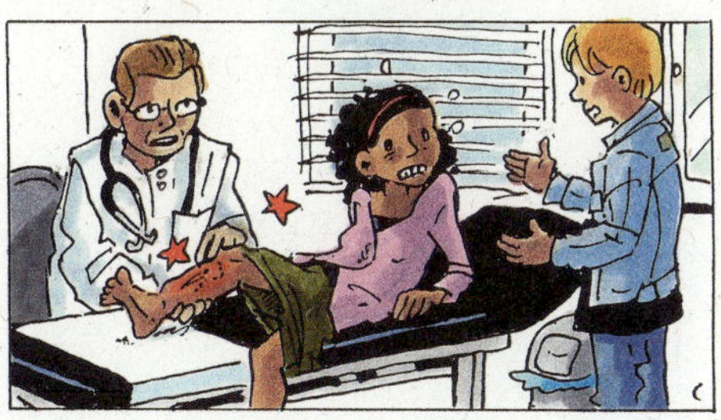

Dr. Schüssler: Wir müssen dein Bein röntgen.
Louise: What was that?

Niko: ______________________________

____

Dr. Schüssler: Du hast eine schwere Prellung am Bein, aber es ist nicht gebrochen.

Niko: ______________________________

____

Packungsbeilage: *Tragen Sie die Salbe morgens und abends auf. Legen Sie einen Verband an.*
Louise: How often do I have to use this cream?

Niko: ______________________________

____

B9 Say it in English

Match the German and the English sentences.

1	Mach dir keine Gedanken.
2	Mach nicht so ein Theater!
3	Na, junger Mann, was ist denn bei dir nicht in Ordnung?
4	Du musst Salbe auftragen.
5	Ich fühle mich schrecklich.
6	Es tut furchtbar weh, wenn ich versuche zu laufen.

A	It hurts terribly when I try to walk.
B	I feel awful.
C	Now, young man, what's wrong with you?
D	Don't worry.
E	You have to put on some cream.
F	Don't make such a fuss!

1	
2	
3	
4	
5	
6	

B10 Your left foot

a) What are you able to do with your left foot? Find out at home and tick your answers.

Are you able to ...	yes	no
pick up things from the floor with your left foot?		
draw pictures with your left foot?		
eat with your left foot?		
type on the computer with your left foot?		
switch on the TV with your left foot?		

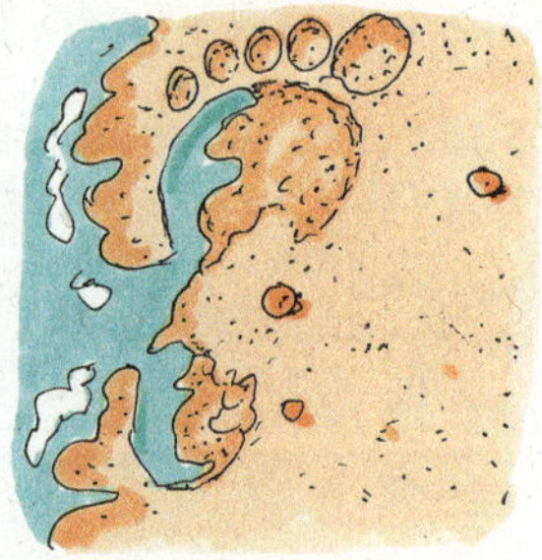

b) What else are you able to do with your left foot? What aren't you able to do with it? Find out and make notes.

____

____

____

c) Tell the class what you have found out.

B11 The life of Christy Brown

a) Look at TB B9 again and answer the questions.

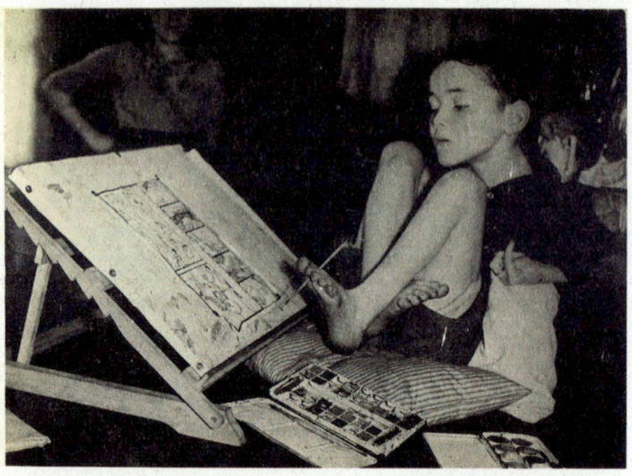

1. How many people were there in Christy's family? ______________________________

how to read TB p.144

2. Which country was the Brown family from? ______________________________
3. What was Christy's father's job? ______________________________
4. Who was the first person to notice that Christy could not move properly? ______________________________
5. Where did Christy learn to control his body a little? ______________________________
6. What made Christy famous? ______________________________
7. What is *My Left Foot?* ______________________________

Work with a partner or in a group. Discuss these questions and make notes in your exercise book. Then compare your ideas in class.

1. Why did Christy learn a lot of things although he never went to school? Find reasons in the text. Then add other possible reasons you can think of.
2. Who do you think helped Christy the most to become an artist? Give reasons.

B12 Choose

1. Read TB B9 again. What was not possible for Christy Brown? What was difficult, but possible for him? Were there also things that were easy for him? Note down your ideas and present them in class.
2. Find some examples of Christy Brown's drawings on the Internet. Print them and make a display or show them on the whiteboard.
3. Watch some scenes of the film 'My Left Foot' on the Internet (09:40 – 14:32). Then tell the class what happens in the scenes. What do you learn about Christy's abilities and disabilities?

B13 Target task: Waiting room stories

a) Listen to a scene in a waiting room. Who is talking? Tick the right people.
New words: rake – *Harke;* tines – *Zinken*

CD 64

b) Listen again. What can you find out about the people's health problems? Take notes.

how to listen TB p. 143

____

____

____

____

____

____

Tipp
Hört euch den Dialog noch einmal an, bevor ihr mit TB B11 anfangt.

c) Work with a partner. Summarise the people's stories in German. Tell one story each.

how to mediate TB p. 145

Tipp
Du kannst die Radiosendung zweimal anhören.

Auf Seite 21 kannst du noch einmal nachlesen, wie du mit den *Test-yourself*-Seiten arbeitest. Die Lösungen findest du ab Seite 124.

T1 Listening: Successful fundraising

CD 67

Read the questions. Then listen to a radio show and tick the right answers.

1. What kind of fundraising event did they organise at South Park School?
   - ☐ a bike-a-thon ☐ a marathon ☐ a walk-a-thon
2. How many sponsors did Fiona have? ☐ five ☐ six ☐ eleven
3. How many sponsors did Abdullah have? ☐ eight ☐ 15 ☐ 18
4. When did the event take place?
   - ☐ last Saturday ☐ last Sunday ☐ last Monday

von 8

CD 67

Read the questions. Then listen to a radio show and tick the right answers.

1. What kind of fundraising event did they organise at South Park School?
   - ☐ a bike-a-thon ☐ a marathon ☐ a walk-a-thon
2. How much money did the pupils raise? ☐ £8,000 ☐ £18,000 ☐ £80,000
3. How many pupils took part in the event? ☐ 532 ☐ 564 ☐ 604
4. How much money did Abdullah collect? ☐ £23 ☐ £33 ☐ £43
5. What is the school going to use the money for?
   - ☐ a swimming pool ☐ gym equipment ☐ the bathrooms in the gym
   - ☐ computers ☐ books for the library ☐ the partner school in Africa

von 16

CD 67

Read the questions. Then listen to a radio show and tick the right answers.

1. What kind of fundraising event did they organise at South Park School?
   - ☐ a bike-a-thon ☐ a marathon ☐ a walk-a-thon
2. How much money did the pupils raise? ☐ £8,000 ☐ £18,000 ☐ £80,000
3. How many pupils took part in the event? ☐ 532 ☐ 564 ☐ 604
4. How old is Fiona? ☐ 10 ☐ 11 ☐ 12
5. How much money did Fiona collect? ☐ £21 ☐ £25 ☐ £35
6. How much money did Abdullah collect? ☐ £23 ☐ £33 ☐ £43
7. When did the event take place?
   - ☐ last Saturday ☐ last Sunday ☐ last Monday
8. What is the school going to use the money for?
   - ☐ a swimming pool ☐ gym equipment ☐ the bathrooms in the gym
   - ☐ computers ☐ books for the library ☐ the partner school in Africa

von 22

T2 Reading: Fastest runner ever

Read about Usain Bolt's career.

Usain Bolt is a Jamaican athlete. Many sports experts consider him to be the greatest sprinter of all time.
Usain was born in Jamaica on 21 August 1986 and still lives there. He is 1.95 metres tall and weighs 94 kg. He once said about himself: "When I was young, I didn't really think about anything other than sports." He played different sports until some coaches noticed his sprinting talent and convinced him to improve this athletic ability. Usain became famous in 2008 when he took part in the Olympic Games in Beijing and won the 100 metres, 200 metres and 4 x 100 metres, all in world record times. At the 2012 Olympic Games in London and the 2016 Olympic Games in Rio he won three gold medals in the same events. Usain has also won eleven world championship[1] titles. His personal best was 9.58 seconds in the 100 metres and it is the fastest time any athlete has ever run. The media often call Usain 'Lightning Bolt'[2] because of his last name and his speed[3].

[1] world championship – *Weltmeisterschaft;* [2] lightning bolt – *Blitz, Blitzschlag;* [3] speed – *Geschwindigkeit*

Answer the questions.

1. What country is Usain Bolt from? ____________________
2. What is his sport? ____________________
3. How many times has Usain won three Olympic gold medals? ____________________
4. What is his fastest time? ____________________

von 8

Tick the correct sentences.

1. Usain Bolt has British nationality. ☐
2. He is 1.94 metres tall and weighs 95 kg. ☐
3. He won three gold medals at three Olympic Games. ☐
4. He has been very successful at some world championships, too. ☐
5. Usain's personal best is also the fastest time any person has ever run. ☐

von 10

Answer the questions.

1. In which country does Usain Bolt live? ____________________
2. How heavy is he? ____________________
3. When did he turn 30? ____________________
4. When did he win three Olympic gold medals for the second time? ____________________
5. Why is the nickname[4] 'Lightning Bolt' a play on words[5]? ____________________

____

von 10

[4] nickname – *Spitzname;* [5] play on words – *Wortspiel*

Tipp
Nehmt euren Dialog auf.

T3 Speaking: In the waiting room

Act out parts 1 – 6. **Act out parts 1 – 10.** **Act out the whole dialogue.**

Patient/in A

1 Frage B, was ihm/ihr fehlt.

3 Sage, dass das schlimm klingt.

5 Sage, dass du in Glasscherben getreten bist und dir den Fuß geschnitten hast.

Patient/in B

2 Sage, dass du dir vermutlich den Arm gebrochen hast.

4 Sage, dass es wehtut. Frage dann A, was ihm/ihr fehlt.

6 Sage, dass das auch schlimm ist.

___ von 6

Patient/in A

7 Frage B, wie er/sie sich den Arm gebrochen hat.

9 Drücke dein Mitgefühl aus. Sage dann, dass die Ärztin den Arm von B wahrscheinlich röntgen wird.

Patient/in B

8 Erzähle, dass du im Park Inliner gefahren und gefallen bist.

10 Sage, dass du das auch glaubst und dass noch nie eine Röntgenaufnahme bei dir gemacht wurde.

___ von 10

Patient/in A

11 Sage, dass du hoffst, dass die Ärztin bald für euch frei sein wird.

13 Sage, dass du sogar schon länger wartest. Dann wirst du aufgerufen und sagst, dass du jetzt dran bist. Wünsche B viel Glück und gute Besserung.

Patient/in B

12 Bestätige, dass du das auch hoffst, und ergänze, dass du schon über eine Stunde lang wartest.

14 Bedanke dich und sage, du hoffst, dass die Ärztin A ebenfalls helfen wird.

___ von 14

T4 Writing: Charlene's sport

Use the notes in the box to write about Charlene's sport.

Write five sentences.
Write eight sentences.
Write ten sentences.

- name: Charlene
- sport: gymnastics; Charlene: very good
- member of a girls' team for four years
- training: twice a week; more often before competitions
- special clothes: leotards[1], gym shoes
- favourite discipline[2]: aerobic gymnastics; small groups; perform to music
- three competitions with her team in the last two years; last time: first prize

___ von 10

___ von 16

___ von 20

[1] leotard – *Turnanzug;* [2] discipline – *Disziplin*

T5 Mediation: Useful tips for bake sales

☆ **Say in German what kind of event the tips are about. Then choose three tips and summarise them.**

☾ **Say in German what kind of event the tips are about. Then choose five tips and summarise them.**

☼ **Say in German what kind of event the tips are about. Then summarise them.**

How to plan a bake sale

Organising a bake sale is a good way to raise money for charity and it is also lots of fun. Here are some useful tips:

- Make the cakes and biscuits yourself. Choose simple recipes. Few ingredients mean low costs for you. You can also use cake or brownie mixes.
- Wash your hands before and after baking.
- Go to a bakery and find out how much their cakes are. You can also ask an adult for help with the prices.
- Make price labels on small pieces of paper and stick them to the front of the plates with your cakes and cookies.
- Use a table to make a stall. Cover it with a nice tablecloth.
- Make a big colourful sign to get people's attention.
- Have a box for the money you get. Start with enough change.
- Be very friendly to your customers. Give them time to decide what they want to buy.

von 6

von 10

von 16

Trage die Punkte, die du erreicht hast, in diese Tabelle ein. Achte darauf, wie die Aufgabe gekennzeichnet ist (Stern, Mond oder Sonne). Insgesamt trägst du fünf Ergebnisse ein.

	☆	☾	☼
Listening	____ von 8	____ von 16	____ von 22
Reading	____ von 8	____ von 10	____ von 10
Speaking	____ von 6	____ von 10	____ von 14
Writing	____ von 10	____ von 16	____ von 20
Mediation	____ von 6	____ von 10	____ von 16

Mithilfe dieser Übersichten findest du heraus, wie du bei den einzelnen Aufgaben abgeschnitten hast. Markiere die Felder, die auf dich zutreffen.

	☆			☾			☼		
	Super!	Gut!	Nur Mut!	Super!	Gut!	Nur Mut!	Super!	Gut!	Nur Mut!
Listening	8–6	5–3	2–0	16–12	11–6	5–0	22–18	17–13	12–0
Reading	8–6	5–3	2–0	10–7	6–4	3–0	10–7	6–4	3–0
Speaking	6–5	4–3	2–0	10–7	6–4	3–0	14–11	10–6	5–0
Writing	10–7	6–4	3–0	16–12	11–6	5–0	20–14	13–8	7–0
Mediation	6–5	4–3	2–0	10–7	6–4	3–0	16–12	11–6	5–0

M1 Listening: Doctor, Doctor

CD 68

Listen to these people talking to Dr Ewalski. What's wrong with them? Draw lines.

Mrs Dunn | Delia | Rick | Mr Roy | Darren | Miranda

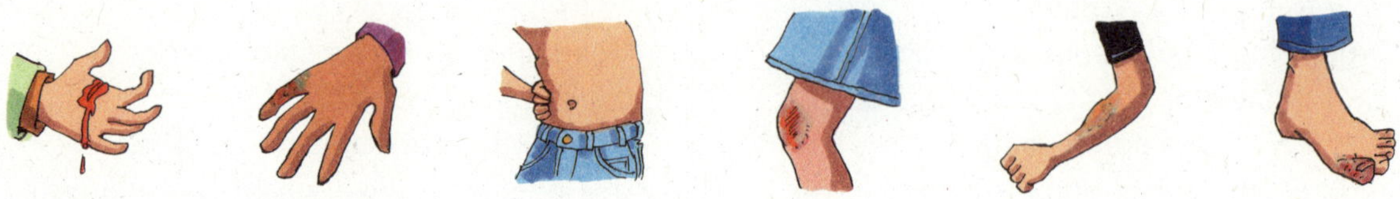

M2 Reading: An accident

Read what Alicia reports about her accident. Then tick the correct sentences.

Last summer, I broke my arm. It happened when I was playing basketball. A girl from the other team pushed me. I fell on my left arm and it hurt a lot. My arm looked really strange and it was swollen. It was 7 pm so I couldn't go to the doctor's. My parents drove me to hospital. There a doctor took an X-ray of my arm. Then he told me that it was broken. The rest of the summer was really boring. I couldn't move my arm for six weeks and I couldn't go swimming or play basketball during that time ...

1. Alicia broke her leg last spring. ☐
2. A girl pushed her when she was playing basketball. ☐
3. It happened in the evening. ☐
4. Alicia's parents drove her to the doctor's. ☐
5. An X-ray showed that her leg was broken. ☐
6. After the accident Alicia couldn't play basketball for six weeks. ☐

M3 Grammar: Fun sports

Complete the sentences with the words from the box.

rope-skipping • walking • doing • watching • running • playing

LiF p. 132 7

1. ______________ a marathon is a challenge.
2. Mila likes ____________________ press-ups.
3. _________________________ to music is fun.
4. Eli is good at ____________________ hockey.
5. _____________ football matches is exciting.
6. Gus enjoys ____________ in the mountains.

M4 Grammar: Faster, slower, ...

Compare the people and things.

fast: sports cars – family cars	dangerous: paragliding – playing football
expensive: bikes – skateboards	slow: skaters – cyclists
lazy: couch pototoes – athletes	cheap: playing basketball – playing golf

Sports cars are faster than ______________________________

____

____

____

____

____

LiF p. 133
8R

M5 Grammar: If you have got a Picasso ...

Look at the pictures and write sentences with 'if'.

sell it for millions of pounds

be very rich

travel around the world

visit lots of famous places

meet interesting people

get invitations to fantastic parties

be in magazines

If you have got a Picasso, you can sell it for millions of pounds.

If you sell it for millions of pounds, you will ______________________________

If you are ______________________________

____

____

____

____

LiF p. 133/4
9R, 10

D1 Get fit!

Do these exercises.

Jump up and down for one minute.
Do 15 press-ups.
Hop on your right foot 20 times. Then do the same on your left foot.
Touch the floor with your fingers. Do this ten times.

D2 Double letters

Complete the words.

CC • EE • FF • LL • MM • PP • SS

O _ _ E R   S W I _ _ E R   D I S C U _ _

P R E _ _   S U _ _ O R T   W H _ _ L

S W O _ _ E N   P R O F E _ _ I O N A L

I _ _ N E _ _   S U _ _ E _ _ F U L

D3 English words, German words, ...

Find words in Theme 3 that are similar to words in German or another language you speak.

English	German	language: ____________
sports	Sport	

D4 Athletic animals

What do you call a dinosaur with a football?

A dinoscore!

What animal is best at hitting a baseball?

A bat!

A1 What a story!

a) Look at TB A1 again. Why is it an adventure story? Tick your answers.

- ☐ Robinson is a brave[1] hero.
- ☐ He is a normal person.
- ☐ The story takes place on a faraway[2] island.
- ☐ Not much happens in the story, but you learn a lot about nature and animals.
- ☐ Robinson is in many very dangerous and difficult situations on the island.
- ☐ He was in many dangerous situations before his life on the island.
- ☐ Everything on the island is unknown to him and he learns how to help himself.

[1] brave – *tapfer, mutig;* [2] faraway – *fern, weit entfernt*

b) Talk to a partner about your ideas. Give reasons for your answers.

I think 'Robinson Crusoe' is an adventure story because ...

I agree.

I don't think so because ...

A2 Sound check

a) Listen to the simple past forms and repeat them.

CD 70

	/t/	/d/	/ɪd/
followed			
tasted			
asked			
boarded			
passed			
sailed			

	/t/	/d/	/ɪd/
collected			
showed			
expected			
looked			
arrived			
missed			

b) Tick the correct sound.

c) Listen to the CD and check your answers.

CD 71

Write down at least three more simple past forms for each sound. Then compare your lists with a partner.

/t/: ______________________________

/d/: ______________________________

/ɪd/: ______________________________

A3 Robinson's feelings

a) How do you think Robinson felt in these situations? Note down your ideas.

excited • glad • happy • proud • surprised • ...

exhausted • helpless • homesick • lonely • sad • scared • seasick • shocked • unhappy • ...

situation	Robinson felt ...
Robinson's ship hit some rocks in the Caribbean.	
Robinson dragged himself onto the beach of an island.	
He didn't see any other people on the island.	
He tamed wild goats and grew wheat.	
He walked along the beach in the evening.	
He saw a group of cannibals with a prisoner.	

wordbank feelings TB p. 161

b) Write about your ideas.

LiF p. 134 11R

When Robinson's ship hit some rocks in the Caribbean, he felt ______

When Robinson ______

When he ______

______

______

______

c) Compare your ideas with a partner and give reasons.

I think Robinson felt ... when he ... because ...

Maybe he also felt ... because ...

- **Look at TB A1 again. Write about Robinson's feelings ...**

  in three other situations. **in five other situations.**

When Robinson ______ he felt ______

______

______

______

______

A4 Life on the island

a) Fill in the simple past forms of the verbs.

arrive • be • build • call • cook • drink • eat • go • have • kill • live • make • rescue • sail • spend • start • teach • watch

Robinson ____________ a new life on an island in the Caribbean. He ____________ there for many years. He ____________ bananas and potatoes and he ____________ water and milk. He ____________ animals with a gun[1] and ____________ them on a fire. He also ____________ some useful things. For example he ____________ a raft. Sometimes Robinson ____________ lonely. Then one day he ____________ a group of cannibals on the beach and he ____________ one of their prisoners. He ____________ him Man Friday. From then on, the two men ____________ a lot of time together. They often ____________ fishing. They also ____________ a lot of adventures. Robinson ____________ Man Friday to speak English. Many years later an English ship ____________ by. In 1687 Robinson and Man Friday ____________ in England.

LiF p. 134 11R

1 gun – *Schusswaffe*

b) Listen to the CD and check your text.

CD 72

c) Look at the verb forms in the text. Mark the regular and the irregular simple past forms in different colours.

Fill in the infinitives of at least three regular and three irregular verbs. Then swap books with a partner. He or she fills in the simple past forms.

regular verbs	
infinitive	**simple past**

irregular verbs	
infinitive	**simple past**

Tipp
Trage Verben ein, die nicht auf dieser Seite verwendet werden.

A5 Questions for Man Friday

a) People also had lots of questions for Man Friday. Here are some. Unscramble ...

☆ **four questions.** ☾ **six questions.** ☼ **all the questions.**

1. cannibals • did • Why • the • you • catch • ?

____

LiF p. 134/5 11R, 12

2. you • Robinson • How • rescue • did • ?

____

3. afraid • Robinson • Were • of • you • ?

____

4. celebrate • you • together • Did • Christmas • ?

____

5. English • first • were • words • What • your • ?

____

6. on • like • island • Did • living • the • you • ?

____

7. call • Why • Man Friday • you • Robinson • did • ?

____

8. didn't • island • Why • stay • the • on • you • ?

____

CD 74

b) Listen to the CD and check your questions.

c) Match the answers with the questions that you have unscrambled.

☐ "Please" and "thank you".

☐ Yes, I was at first. But Robinson was really nice to me. So I lost my fear.

☐ Robinson wanted to go home and I didn't want to stay on the island all alone.

☐ Because he met me on a Friday.

☐ They wanted to kill me and eat me.

☐ He fired at the cannibals with his gun.

☐ Yes, I did. It was a beautiful place.

☐ Yes, we did. I became a Christian and Robinson told me everything about the festival.

Write down questions that go with these answers.

1. ____________________ I taught him how to fish, for example.

2. ____________________ Because he was wounded.

3. ____________________ On 19th December 1686.

With a partner, write down more interesting questions for Man Friday and think of good answers. Read out your dialogues in class.

A6 Island life

a) Listen to the poem and read along.

CD 76

Set out on your way to the island,
That's where you see and smell the sea.
Say farewell to the life of the mainland,
And discover a new way to be.

Walking up and down the beach,
You breathe in the salty air,
Here your troubles have no reach,
And you'll forget your every care.

You stand in the water and look,
At the fish swimming over your feet,
And with the world as your book,
You read the waves by their beat.

Boats and ferries come and go,
People come here just to rest.
You watch the sunset and you know
That island life is the best.

The sun doesn't always shine,
The rain can last for hours.
But you always feel just fine,
The beauty never sours.

You won't return to the mainland,
This is your home now.
This sea, these winds, this island,
This is your home now.

b) Look up new words.

c) Read the poem again. What does the speaker like about the island? Talk to a partner.

d) Do you like the poem? Why or why not? Compare your ideas in class.

A7 What is home?

Work with a partner. Choose at least two of these sayings each. Use your own words to say in English what they are about.

how to mediate TB p. 145

Ein Haus ist noch kein Zuhause.

Vier eigene Wände machen einen Menschen frei.

Alles Leben draußen ist nur wie ein Schlafen in Kleidern. Daheim erst liegt man im Bett.

Nicht da ist man daheim, wo man seinen Wohnsitz hat, sondern wo man verstanden wird.

Wer daheim bleibt, muss den Heimweg nicht suchen.

Wer sich überall zu Hause fühlt, ist nirgends daheim.

Dein Heim kann dir die Welt ersetzen, doch nie die Welt dein Heim.

A8 Target task: Useful things on a lonely island

CD 77

a) Listen to a group of British pupils discussing what they would need on a lonely island. What things do they talk about? What are their ideas? Take notes in the grid.

how to listen TB p. 143

thing	Why is it useful?	Why is it not really necessary or not even useful?

b) Compare your notes in a group.

c) Do you agree with the ideas? Can you think of any other ideas? Discuss.

I agree that ... is useful because ...

I think you can also use ... to ...

I don't think ... is useful ... because ...

...

d) Add your ideas to the grid.

e) Do you think other things are more important? Look at the pictures in TB A11 and discuss.

Use your results when working on TB A11.

B1 Hard times and good times

a) What do you do when you have problems? Complete the sentences. You can use ideas from the box or your own ideas.

call my best friend • cry • eat lots of sweets • go to the park • hide somewhere • listen to sad music • run away • shout loudly • stay in my room and lock the door • talk to my parents • be alone • …

When I feel sad I want to ______________________________

When I feel shy I would love to ______________________________

When I'm angry I ______________________________

When I feel lonely ______________________________

When I'm worried ______________________________

When I'm annoyed ______________________________

When I'm scared ______________________________

b) ☾ Write about times when you feel good, happy, pleased, excited and proud in your exercise book.

I feel good when …

☼ Write about three or more situations in which you felt great, excited or proud in your exercise book. Why did you feel that way? What did you do? Show your text to your partner and read his or her text.

I felt great when … because …

B2 Problem page

Look at TB B2 again and tick right or wrong.

	right	wrong
1. Three teenagers who wrote letters are 13 years old.	☐	☐
2. Charlotte ran away from home.	☐	☐
3. Charlotte's parents have met her boyfriend and won't accept him.	☐	☐
4. Joe has received some terrible emails.	☐	☐
5. Saya's sister thinks Saya is lazy.	☐	☐
6. Carl's family has got a big house.	☐	☐
7. Sarah says that Carl can't take a dog to school with him.	☐	☐
8. Tom forgets everything when teachers ask him questions at school.	☐	☐
9. Sarah's advice for Tom is not to think about what others think.	☐	☐

☾ ☼ Correct the wrong sentences in your exercise book.

B3 Problems

What are these teenagers saying about their problems? Number the speech bubbles.

1 Logan

2 Mason

3 Carys

4 Oliver

5 Sally

6 Freya

7 Phyllis

8 Gemma

☐ *I'm really bad at maths and so worried about the tests.*

☐ *I really like this girl, but she always ignores me.*

☐ *My skin looks terrible. I've got so many spots. I'm so unhappy.*

☐ *My mum always tells me to tidy up my room. But I like it the way it is.*

☐ *My best friend stopped talking to me and I don't know why.*

☐ *My dad won't let me go out with my friends. He says I'm too young.*

☐ *I don't get much pocket money. I can't buy clothes or go to the cinema like some of my friends.*

For one picture there is no speech bubble. Write down what the teenager in that picture might say.

____

____

____

B4 There's help

☆ **Look at B3 again and match the teenagers' names with the advice.**

1	Logan,	A	why don't you try to get a Saturday job?	1	
2	Mason,	B	you should talk to your teacher about your problem.	2	
3	Carys,	C	it helps to put your things away after you've used them.	3	
4	Oliver,	D	explain to your father how you feel.	4	
5	Sally,	E	it's YOUR style. So this isn't your problem, it's your mum's.	5	
6	Freya,	F	can you ask another friend what the problem could be?	6	
7	Phyllis,	G	you shouldn't use any make-up or wash your face with soap.	7	
8	Gemma,	H	you could find out about her hobbies and then try to talk to her.	8	

☾ **Give advice to the teenagers in B3. Use the phrases in the box or your own ideas.**

do your maths homework with friends • try to talk to her in the cafeteria • explain to your dad how terrible you feel • tidy one part of your room every day • ask your mum nicely to let you choose your own style • stop eating sweets and spicy food • sell some old things • write a nice text message to her and ask what's wrong • ...

Logan, why don't you ______

Mason, have you tried to ______

Carys, perhaps you could ______

Oliver, it would be helpful ______

Sally, ______

______

______

______

☼ **Choose a teenager from B3. What would *you* say to him or her? Give some advice, too.**

______

______

______

______

______

______

B5 Girls' talk

CD 81

a) Vanessa and Gillian are looking at the letters to Sarah. Listen to the CD. Number the headlines in the order the girls are talking about them.

- [ ] Cyber bullying
- [ ] I'm so shy
- [ ] My love is a secret
- [ ] Dad says: No dog
- [ ] I hate my sister

b) ☆ Listen again and tick the right answers.

1. Who would like to have a dog?	☐ Gillian	☐ Vanessa
2. Who would like to have a sister?	☐ Gillian	☐ Vanessa

Read the questions. Then listen again and answer …
☾ two questions in your exercise book. ☼ all the questions in your exercise book.

1. Which problem is also Vanessa's problem?
2. Why does Gillian say "Oh, stop it, Vanessa!"?
3. What do the girls say about bullying at their school?
4. Who wants to have a sister, and why?

B6 Choose

1. Bring a German magazine for teenagers to class. Show the problem page and tell your classmates in English what the letters are about.
2. A lot of singers and bands sing about problems. Bring one song to class, play it and say what it is about. It can be a German or an English song.
3. Have you seen a film or read a book about teenagers' problems? Give a short talk in class about the film or the book you have chosen. Who are the characters? What are their problems? Why do you like the story?

B7 Little words

a) Match the verbs with the prepositions.

rely • break • sort • feel sorry • talk • cool	down • for • on • out • over • up

__________ __________

__________ __________

__________ __________

b) Write sentences with … ☆ two of the phrases. ☾ four of the phrases. ☼ all the phrases. Write them into your exercise book.

B8 Charlie's family

Look at TB B4 again. Then close your textbook and match the facts with the family members. Draw lines.

Mr Batson

Josephine

Sharon

- is Charlie's younger sister
- is a trainee nurse
- works in a supermarket
- didn't have a good school report
- works the early shift
- does the housework and the cooking
- does a 12-hour shift
- can't go back to ballet lessons
- is an engineer
- thinks about Lisa all the time
- is out of work at the moment

Mrs Batson

Charlie

Look at TB B4 again. Then read this text and correct the wrong words and phrases.

Every ~~afternoon~~ morning Mr Batson checks some magazines and looks for cars on the Internet because he is out of work at the moment. He is a lorry driver. About once a month he walks down to the job centre. Mrs Batson works in a shopping centre. First she has to fill up boxes and then she sits at the information desk. Her boss is very nice and makes life easy for her. Josephine is a doctor at St Mary's Hospital in Notting Hill. She has a 14-hour shift. Her boyfriend likes to ride his bike. Sharon is 12 and often cleans her room. She'd love to go back to hip hop lessons but they are too expensive. Charlie loves playing hockey. He thinks about his goldfish all the time. His last school report was really good.

Answer these questions. Write more than one sentence for each answer.

1. What does Mr Batson do to find a new job?
2. Why is it hard for Mrs Batson to work at the supermarket?
3. What is Josephine's life like?
4. What does Sharon like and what doesn't she like?
5. What is important to Charlie?

B9 Would you love or hate it?

What can you say in these situations? Use the phrases in the box.

I'd like to • I'd love to • I'd hate to • I'd rather

1. You very much want to have an ice cream.

I'd love to have an ice cream.

2. Your friend wants to go to the cinema, but you think it is better to go to the swimming pool.

I'd ______________________________

3. Some foreign students tell you that they have to take twelve maths tests each school year. You think that is terrible.

____

4. You are tired and you dream of lying on a beautiful tropical beach.

____

5. You have to give a talk in science, but you wish you could give a talk in history.

____

6. You think it would be quite nice to take guitar lessons.

____

B10 The Batsons' situation

a) Fill in the simple past forms.

found • had • could • stopped

1. If the Batsons __________ more money, Mrs Batson would stop working at the supermarket.
2. Charlie would do better at school if he __________ thinking about Lisa so often.
3. If Mr Batson __________ a new job, he would no longer have time to do the housework.
4. Sharon would be really happy if she __________ take ballet lessons again.

LiF p. 136 13

b) Fill in the conditional forms.

would show • would like • would take • would be

1. If the job centre offered Mr Batson a job, he __________ it.
2. Mr and Mrs Batson __________ pleased if Charlie had better school reports.
3. If Lisa came to London again, Charlie __________ her lots of nice places.
4. Mrs Batson __________ her job better if her boss was friendlier.

B11 What would be different?

a) **Fill in the correct forms of the verbs in the box. The verbs are in the right order.**

be • can • meet • worry • not have

1. If Mr Batson ______________ younger, it would perhaps be easier for him to find a new job.
2. If Mrs Batson didn't work the early shift, she ______________ get up later.
3. Josephine ______________ her boyfriend more often if she worked shorter shifts.
4. Mrs Batson ______________ less if Josephine's boyfriend didn't drive fast cars.
5. If the Batsons ______________ money problems, Charlie could go to the pony camp in Scotland again next summer.

LiF p. 136
13

b) **Listen to the CD and check your sentences.**

CD 83

B12 Target task: Ways to give a helping hand

a) **Listen to three scenes about problems at school and take notes.**

CD 84

name	his or her problem	how the person's classmate gives a helping hand
Logan		
Tareq		
Maya		

b) **Do you think the children's classmates were able to give a helping hand? Look at your notes again and then discuss your ideas in class.**

Tipp
Hört euch die Dialoge noch einmal an, bevor ihr TB B9 bearbeitet.

Auf Seite 21 kannst du noch einmal nachlesen, wie du mit den *Test-yourself*-Seiten arbeitest. Die Lösungen findest du ab Seite 125.

T1 Listening: Stuart's worries

CD 91

☆ **a) Listen to Stuart talking to a school counsellor. What is his problem?**

- ☐ He doesn't know how to help his friend Ibrahim with his presentations.
- ☐ He gets very nervous when he has to give a presentation.
- ☐ He is really bad at geography and can't give a presentation next week.

b) Listen again and tick what you hear.

- ☐ "Can you help me, please?"
- ☐ "Sometimes I can't talk at all."
- ☐ "I could try it out."
- ☐ "There's not much I can do."

von 6

CD 92

☾ **a) Listen to Stuart talking to a school counsellor. What is his problem?**

Stuart gets very nervous when ______________________________

b) Listen again. What advice does the school counsellor give Stuart? Tick the things she says are helpful.

The school counsellor says that …

- ☐ Stuart has to stop the kids who are laughing.
- ☐ Stuart can practise presentations with Ibrahim.
- ☐ Stuart can practise presentations in front of a mirror.
- ☐ Stuart can ask Ibrahim to make a video when he is practising.

von 6

CD 92

☼ **a) Listen to Stuart talking to a school counsellor. What is his problem?**

____

b) Listen again. What advice does the school counsellor give Stuart? Tick the things she says are helpful.

The school counsellor says that …

- ☐ Stuart has to stop the kids who are laughing.
- ☐ Stuart can practise presentations with Ibrahim.
- ☐ Stuart can practise presentations in front of a mirror.
- ☐ Stuart can ask Ibrahim to make a video when he is practising.
- ☐ Stuart can ask his parents to take photos of him.
- ☐ Stuart can learn his presentations by heart.
- ☐ Stuart can come again on Monday and practise the geography presentation with her.

von 8

T2 Reading: The real Robinson

Read about the life of Alexander Selkirk.

Alexander Selkirk was born in Lower Largo, Scotland, in 1676. He worked as a sailor on a ship called *Cinque Ports* that left Ireland for South America in 1703. In 1704, the *Cinque Ports* arrived at Mas a Tierra, an island in the South Pacific about 600 km west of Chile. Alexander had a problem with the captain and decided to stay on the island.
At first Alexander felt scared and lonely, but then he started to explore[1] the island and discovered fresh water and wild vegetables. He also found goats and always had enough milk and meat. Alexander had some tools[2] and built two small houses: one for cooking and one for sleeping. He often read the Bible[3]. Once he fell and hurt himself badly. He couldn't move for a whole day. Two times he had to hide[4] when Spanish ships came to the island because Spain was at war[5] with Britain. Four years and four months passed until finally a British ship called *Duke* came to the island and rescued Alexander. In October 1711, he arrived back in England and people were very interested in his stories about the island.
A few years later Alexander started to work as a sailor again. In 1721 he went on a voyage to Africa, but he fell ill on the ship and died.
After hearing Alexander's story, Daniel Defoe wrote his famous book *Robinson Crusoe*. Mas a Tierra is now called Robinson Crusoe Island. Today about 600 people live there.

[1] explore – *erforschen, erkunden;* [2] tool – *Werkzeug;* [3] the Bible – *die Bibel;* [4] hide – *sich verstecken;* [5] at war – *im Krieg*

Cross out the wrong information.

1. Alexander Selkirk was born **in 1679/in 1676**.
2. He died **in 1712/in 1721**.
3. He lived on a lonely island **for four years and four months/for five years and six months**.
4. Today the island is called **Mas a Tierra/Robinson Crusoe Island**.

von 8

Tick the right information.

1. Alexander was born	☐ in England.	☐ in Scotland.	☐ in Ireland.
2. His ship was called	☐ Lower Largo.	☐ Mas a Tierra.	☐ *Cinque Ports*.
3. On the island he drank	☐ water and milk.	☐ only fresh water.	☐ only goat milk.
4. The *Duke* rescued him	☐ in 1704.	☐ in 1711.	☐ in 1721.
5. The island is now called	☐ Selkirk Island.	☐ Robinson Crusoe Island.	☐ Mas a Tierra.

von 10

Answer the questions.

1. How old was Alexander when he arrived on the island? ______________________
2. Where is the island? ______________________
3. What did Alexander eat and drink there? ______________________
4. What did he use his two houses for? ______________________
5. What were dangerous situations for him on the island? ______________________

____

von 10

Tipp
Ihr könnt euren Dialog aufnehmen oder vor der Klasse vorführen.

T3 Speaking: Problems between children and parents

Work with a partner. Choose one situation and act out a dialogue.

- ☆ **Each of you speaks at least four times in the dialogue.**
- ☾ **Each of you speaks at least five times in the dialogue.**
- ☼ **Each of you speaks at least six times in the dialogue.**

von 8

von 10

von 12

T4 Writing: Josephine's day

Use the notes in the box to write about Josephine Batson's day.

- ☆ **Write five sentences. You can choose.**
- ☾ **Write eight sentences. You can choose.**
- ☼ **Write ten sentences.**

- get up early, only small breakfast
- hospital: in Paddington, far from Hendon
- take underground to work
- buy newspaper on way to station
- read on train
- always very busy at work
- sunny days: lunch in park near hospital
- love job although often tired
- evening: help parents around the house
- weekend: meet boyfriend

Tipp
Benutze die richtigen Verbformen. Denk an das -*s* in der 3. Person.

von 10

von 16

von 20

T5 Mediation: Holidays on the Isle of Wight

Listen to Annabelle telling Mila about her holiday on the Isle of Wight. What can tourists do on the island? Note down in German what you can find out. Note down …

CD 93

☆ **three activities for tourists.** ☾ **four activities for tourists.** ☼ **six activities for tourists.**

Auf der Isle of Wight können Touristen …

- ______________________________
____
____
____
____
____
____
____
____

☆ ___ von 6

☾ ___ von 8

☼ ___ von 12

Trage die Punkte, die du erreicht hast, in diese Tabelle ein. Achte darauf, wie die Aufgabe gekennzeichnet ist (Stern, Mond oder Sonne). Insgesamt trägst du fünf Ergebnisse ein.

	☆	☾	☼
Listening	___ von 6	___ von 6	___ von 8
Reading	___ von 8	___ von 10	___ von 10
Speaking	___ von 8	___ von 10	___ von 12
Writing	___ von 10	___ von 16	___ von 20
Mediation	___ von 6	___ von 8	___ von 12

Mithilfe dieser Übersichten findest du heraus, wie du bei den einzelnen Aufgaben abgeschnitten hast. Markiere die Felder, die auf dich zutreffen.

	☆			☾			☼		
	Super!	Gut!	Nur Mut!	Super!	Gut!	Nur Mut!	Super!	Gut!	Nur Mut!
Listening	6–5	4–3	2–0	6–5	4–3	2–0	8–6	5–3	2–0
Reading	8–6	5–3	2–0	10–7	6–4	3–0	10–7	6–4	3–0
Speaking	8–6	5–3	2–0	10–7	6–4	3–0	12–9	8–5	4–0
Writing	10–7	6–4	3–0	16–12	11–6	5–0	20–14	13–8	7–0
Mediation	6–5	4–3	2–0	8–6	5–3	2–0	12–9	8–5	4–0

M1 Listening: Teenagers' problems

CD 94

Listen to four teenagers. What do they say about their problems? Draw lines.

	My life is so boring because I can't go anywhere.
Evie	I'm not allowed to go to the cinema or go shopping on my own.
Tyler	My mum wants me to meet the 'new man in her life'.
Seth	I always have to look after my little sister.
Lexi	My parents are getting divorced.
	I hate cooking but I have to help my mum make dinner every night.

M2 Reading: Alone on an island

a) Read the texts.

Cormac: I think you need an axe, a rope, a spade and matches on a lonely island. Then you can build a boat and a house, maybe even a tree house. A toothbrush is also important because you can't go to the dentist. You don't have to bring any food because there are lots of fruit trees on tropical islands and you can also catch fish.

Louise: It is necessary to have a first aid kit, a knife to kill animals and a packet of seeds on a lonely island. Food and medicine are the most important things to survive. Matches are quite useful, too. Then you can easily make a fire and cook your food on it. You can also use a fire to signal to a ship or helicopter.

Kirsty: You have to drink a lot of fresh water when it is hot, so a plastic bottle or a pot to collect rainwater is helpful. You also have to protect your eyes and skin. That's why sunglasses and sunscreen are important. I would like to have some good books and my guitar with me, too. I wouldn't feel so lonely if I could read and play music.

b) Read the questions. Then tick the right names.

Who ...	Cormac	Louise	Kirsty
1. ... would like to have books on a lonely island?	☐	☐	☐
2. ... mentions a toothbrush?	☐	☐	☐
3. ... says that sunscreen is important?	☐	☐	☐
4. ... thinks that matches are useful?	☐	☐	☐
5. ... finds a bottle or a pot helpful to collect rainwater?	☐	☐	☐
6. ... doesn't think you have to bring any food?	☐	☐	☐
7. ... would use a knife to kill animals?	☐	☐	☐

M3 Grammar: Man Friday's story

a) Mark all the simple past forms.

I lived on a very beautiful island with my family. One day I walked to the beach. Suddenly I saw a ship. Some cannibals climbed out of it. They kidnapped me and brought me to another island. I was extremely scared. Suddenly I heard a noise. A white man came and rescued me. At first I couldn't talk to him because I didn't speak English. But then he taught me to speak English. I showed him how to fish and use plants as medicine.

LiF p. 134 11R

b) Write down the infinitives of the simple past forms from a).

____

M4 Grammar: A terrible day

Match the questions with the answers and write them down.

Who was in a very bad mood?

How long did Mrs Batson work?

When did Mrs Batson get up yesterday?

What did she do when she got home?

Why did a customer get angry?

Where did she walk after breakfast?

Questions	Answers
1. ______________________ ______________________	At 6 o'clock as usual.
2. ______________________ ______________________	To the supermarket.
3. ______________________ ______________________	Her boss.
4. ______________________ ______________________	Because there were no pineapples.
5. ______________________ ______________________	She worked for 8.5 hours until half past three.
6. ______________________ ______________________	She cooked dinner and cleaned the kitchen.

LiF p. 134/5 11R, 12

D1 Where?

Write down where you can see the animals and things.

1. A brown dog: ____________________
2. Two cups of yoghurt: ____________________
3. A raft: ____________________
4. Inline skates: ____________________
5. A school report: ____________________
6. A message in a bottle: ____________________

D2 Two letters

Complete the words.

AI • EA • EI • IE • IO • OY

B R _ _ K

A F R _ _ D

R E C _ _ V E

V E R S _ _ N

W _ _ G H T

O P I N _ _ N

E X P E R _ _ N C E

B _ _ F R _ _ N D

D3 What is it?

Complete the words.

1. The ocean between Europe, Africa and America: A _ _ _ n _ _ _
2. You use it to make bottles and toys, for example: p _ _ _ _ _ _
3. You use them to light candles or to make a fire: _ _ t _ _ _ _
4. A fact about your life that you don't tell others: _ _ c _ _ _

D4 Scrambled words

Unscramble the words. They all have to do with Robinson Crusoe's story.

romts ______	osiral ______	nildas ______
kercw ______	Fydira ______	berbiCana ______
banalcins ______	ensipror ______	terednavu ______

D5 A joke

Do you think this is funny?

Two frogs sat on Robinson Crusoe's back. One said to the other: "I have to go now, but let's meet again on Friday!"

A1 An amazing museum

Look at the information about MOSI in TB A1 again. Then tick right or wrong.

	right	wrong
1. You can make a video and see it in the Revolution Manchester display.	☐	☐
2. 'Cottonopolis' is a collection of cotton-making machines.	☐	☐
3. The Victorian sewer is dark and it smells.	☐	☐
4. You can get a bit wet in the 4D Theatre.	☐	☐
5. You can see an original old AVRO F monoplane at MOSI.	☐	☐
6. 'Baby' is the nickname for the inventor of a famous computer.	☐	☐
7. There is a see-through locomotive that helps you understand how a steam engine works.	☐	☐
8. MOSI offers hands-on science because you can do experiments there.	☐	☐

☼ **Correct the wrong sentences in your exercise book.**

A2 On the train to Manchester

☆ **Read the words and phrases. Then listen to the first part of TB A2. Tick what you can hear.**

CD 2/11 95

- ☐ plane
- ☐ stuff
- ☐ history project
- ☐ books
- ☐ old machines
- ☐ awesome
- ☐ minutes
- ☐ journey

☾ **Read the words and phrases. Then listen to both parts of TB A2. Tick what you can hear.**

CD 2/11 95 2/12 96

- ☐ on the plane
- ☐ MOSI brochure
- ☐ cotton industry
- ☐ history project
- ☐ read a book
- ☐ old machines
- ☐ awesome
- ☐ in four minutes
- ☐ journey
- ☐ next stop
- ☐ the first bus
- ☐ fresh air

☼ **Read the phrases. Then listen to both parts of TB A2. Tick what you can hear.**

CD 2/11 95 2/12 96

- ☐ on the plane to Manchester
- ☐ I'd like to read a book
- ☐ the industrial revolution
- ☐ the Air and Space section
- ☐ the modern machines
- ☐ Sounds awful!
- ☐ in four minutes we will be arriving
- ☐ There he is!
- ☐ next stop
- ☐ only about 20 minutes' walk
- ☐ the first bus
- ☐ Come on, lazy bones, let's walk.

A3 Giving directions in a museum

a) **Read about the National Railway Museum in York. Talk to a partner about what you can see there.**

At the National Railway Museum in York you can see over 100 locomotives and almost 300 other railway vehicles[1]. One of the many highlights in the museum is a replica of the 'Rocket', a famous 19th-century steam locomotive. You can also see modern trains, such as the Japanese Shinkansen and the Eurostar.

[1] vehicle – *Fahrzeug*

Tipp
Übt euren Dialog, bevor ihr ihn in der Klasse vorführt. Ihr könnt ein Wörterbuch benutzen.

b) **Look at this plan of the museum. Work with a partner and act out dialogues.**

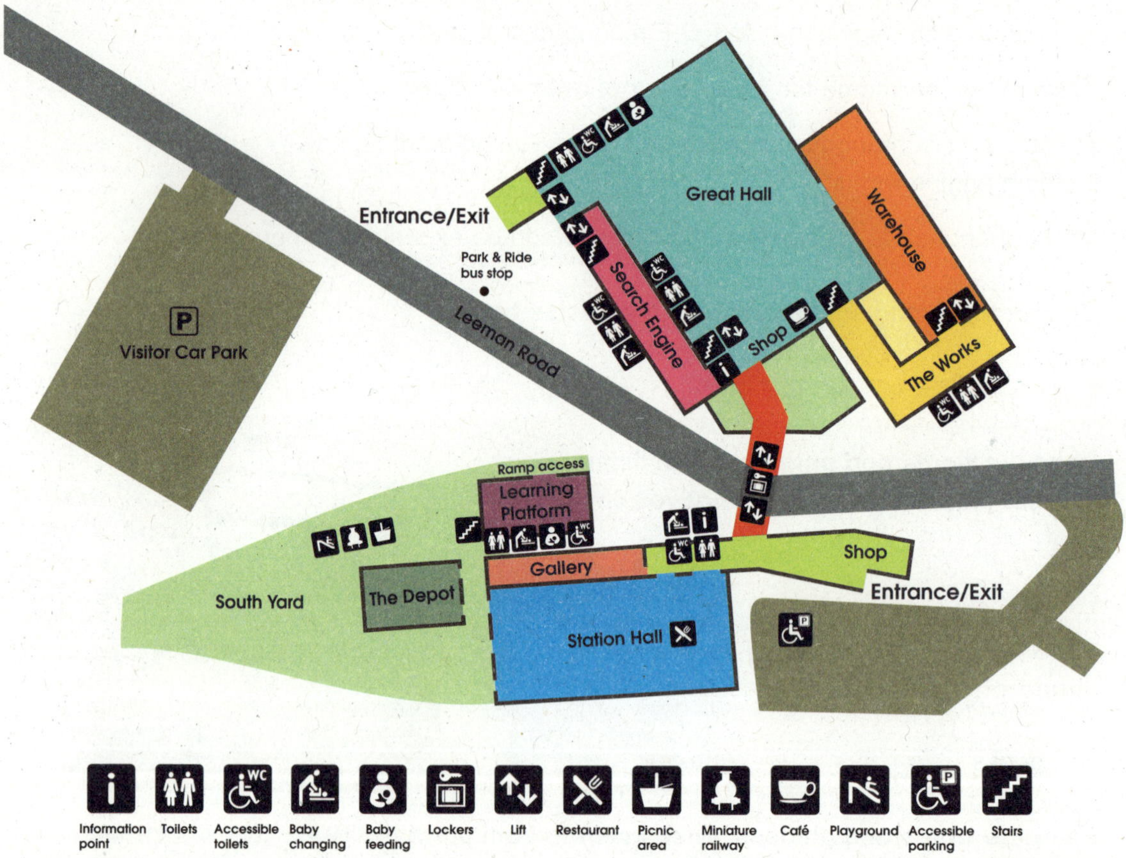

Tipp
Benutzt höfliche Ausdrücke wie *„excuse me"* und *„thank you"*.

☆ **Dialogue 1:** You meet at the entrance to Great Hall.
Partner A: Ask B the way to Station Hall.
Partner B: Give A directions.

Dialogue 2: You meet in the Gallery.
Partner B: Ask A the way to the restaurant.
Partner A: Give B directions.

☾ **Dialogue 1:** You meet at the Works.
Partner A: Ask B the way to Station Hall.
Partner B: Give A directions.

Dialogue 2: You meet at the Learning Platform.
Partner B: Ask A the way to the Depot.
Partner A: Give B directions.

☼ **Dialogue 1:** You meet at the café in Great Hall.
Partner A: You are visiting the museum with your little brother. Ask B the way to the playground.
Partner B: Describe where the playground is and give A directions.

Dialogue 2: You meet at the visitor car park.
Partner B: You don't want to leave your new laptop in the car. Ask A where you can find lockers.
Partner A: Describe where the lockers are and give B directions.

A4 A trip to MOSI

a) Write about David and Gillian's trip to MOSI.

David and Gillian They Gillian	had to	buy be meet cover hold collect	their ears in the Textiles Gallery. information for a history project. train tickets before the trip. their noses in the Victorian sewer. Uncle George at Manchester Piccadilly Station. at the station in London on time.

____

____

____

____

____

____

b) Listen to the CD and check your sentences. CD 97

A5 What Robinson had to do

Robinson Crusoe's life on the island was quite difficult. Write down which things he didn't have and what he had to do because of that.

Robinson didn't have a microwave[1], so he had to ______________________

____

____

____

____

Write about another thing that Robinson didn't have and what he had to do.

____

____

[1] microwave – *Mikrowelle*

A6 Visiting a German museum

You want to take a British friend to the Technik Museum in Speyer. Look at the brochure.

how to mediate TB p.145

Answer your friend's questions.

- Where is the museum?
- What can we see there?

Answer your friend's questions.

- What can we see at the museum?
- How long can we stay there?
- How much are the tickets for us?
- Do you think it's fun for teenagers to go there?

Work with a partner. He or she plays the role of your British friend and asks you questions about the museum. You answer the questions. Make a recording of your dialogue.

Technik MUSEUM SPEYER
Highlights in Luft-, Raum- und Seefahrt!

Das nahe der Innenstadt von Speyer gelegene Technik Museum ist ein fantastisches Ausflugsziel für Jung und Alt. Mehr als 3000 Ausstellungsstücke erwarten Sie hier: Flugzeuge, klassische Automobile, Lokomotiven, U-Boote, Schiffe und viele andere technische Meisterleistungen. Zu den größten Attraktionen zählen eine Boeing 747, die russische Raumfähre BURAN und das voll zugängliche U-Boot U9. Absolut lohnenswert ist auch ein Besuch im IMAX DOME. Hier können Sie auf einer gewaltigen Kuppelleinwand Filme sehen, die Sie in faszinierenden Bildern über Themen aus Natur und Technik informieren.

Technik Museum Speyer
Am Technik Museum 1
67346 Speyer

Wir haben 365 Tage im Jahr geöffnet.
Montag bis Freitag: 9–18 Uhr
Samstag, Sonntag, Feiertage: 9–19 Uhr

Eintrittspreise	Museum	IMAX DOME*	Kombiticket**
Kinder 5–14 J.	12,50 €	7,50 €	15,00 €
Erwachsene	15,00 €	10,00 €	19,00 €

* Preis für eine Vorstellung
** Museumseintritt und eine Vorstellung im IMAX DOME Filmtheater

A7 Sound check

CD 98

a) Listen to the verbs and repeat them.

create • listen • visit • invent • notice • compare • follow • collect • cover • practise • enjoy • explain

b) Which verbs are stressed on the first syllable? Which verbs are stressed on the second syllable? Write them into the lists.

stress on the first syllable	stress on the second syllable

CD 99

c) Listen to the CD and check your lists.

Add one or two verbs to each list.

A8 Target task: Important and useful things

a) Listen to six German pupils talking about things which they want to put in their special class museum. Number the things in the right order.

CD 100

☐ 
football boots

☐ 
bracelet

☐ 
badminton racket and shuttlecock

☐ 
laptop

☐ 
delta kite

☐ 
cuddly toy

b) Why have the pupils chosen these objects? Listen again and take notes ...
☆ about two objects. ☾ about five objects. ☼ about all the objects.

object/objects	why the pupil has chosen it/them

B1 Crossword: Inventions

Fill in the words.

Down ↓

1 You can ride it to school.
2 You use them to light candles.
4 It is a small computer that you can easily carry around with you.
6 You can warm up your food in it very easily.
7 You use it to close jackets.
9 … light bulbs can be used much longer than other light bulbs.

Across →

3 You put this on a letter before you send it.
5 You put it around your wrist and it tells you the time.
8 It can help people who are ill.
10 It cleans your plates.
11 You can watch many different programmes on it.

B2 Invented by kids

Choose one text in TB B3 and take notes in the table.

who	
what (invention)	
where	
when	
how	
further information	

Use your notes for TB B3c).

B3 Active or passive?

a) Mark all the verb forms in the text.

Becky Schroeder invented the Glo-Sheet, a board which is coated with phosphorescent paint. This special paint stores light when it is exposed to daylight. It then glows in the dark. Once a sheet of paper is placed on it, the light shines through and you see the text. In 1974 Becky's invention was patented. It was a huge success. It is used by photographers for their darkrooms, as well as by doctors and nurses in hospitals. Even astronauts use it when their electrical systems are turned down. Becky's bright idea is needed by many people!

b) Write the verb forms into the lists.

active	passive

LiF p. 136 14

c) Which forms are in the past tense? Circle these forms.

B4 Made in …

Write down where these things are made and what they are made of.

Germany, glass • Russia, wood • Japan, paper • China, metal

This snow globe is made in Germany. It is made of glass.

These babushkas

LiF p. 136 14

These origami birds

☾ **Choose two of the things below. Find out what they are made of.**
☼ **Find out what the things below are made of.**

- pencils
- jeans
- DVDs
- perfume
- skateboards

Tell a partner and explain new words.

B5 Interesting, isn't it?

a) Fill in the words from the box. Use each word once.

awarded • called • created • flown • presented • run • sent • sold • used

1. The first hot-air balloon was ______________________ to the public by the Montgolfier brothers in 1783.

2. Inventor Alexander Graham Bell was ____________________ the first American patent for the telephone in 1876.

LiF p. 136 14

3. The first aeroplane was ____________ 'Flyer' and ____________ by its inventors, the Wright Brothers, for the first time in 1903.

4. In the 19th century, steam powered engines were ____________ in British cotton mills.

5. The world's first stored program was ____________ on the computer 'Baby' in 1948.

6. The Internet was ____________ in 1990.

7. The first text message was ___________ in 1994.

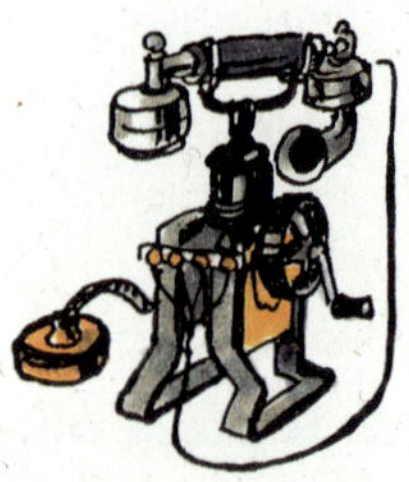

8. Over 1.3 billion smartphones were ____________ worldwide in 2015.

CD 106

b) Listen to the CD and check your sentences.

B6 Invented by ...

a) Look at the pictures and read the table. Then fill in the words for the inventions.

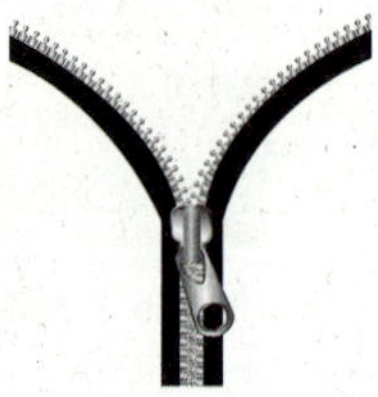

invention	inventor	what for?	when?
	Whitcomb Judson	to help you close your jacket	
	James Russell	to listen to music	
	Thomas Edison	to help you see when it is dark	
	James Chalmer	to put on a letter	
	John Walker	to light a fire	
	Laszlo Biro	to write with	

CD 107

b) Listen to the CD and fill in the dates under 'when?'.

c) Write about the inventions.

The zip was invented in ______ by ______

______

______

______

______

______

Choose one of the inventions in the grid and find out some facts about its history. Give a two-minute talk.

B7 What you need and don't need

a) Fill in the table. Write at least two inventions into each field. Look up new words.

Inventions ...	
I use or need every day	
I often use or need	
I sometimes use or need	
I never use or need	

b) Talk to a partner about the table. Say how often you use or need things and why.

I use my mobile every day because I text a lot.

I sometimes need medicine when I'm ill.

B8 Word families

Complete the lists.

adjective	noun
natural	
	electricity
different	
	success
dark	

verb	noun
patent	
	paint
charge	
	driver
use	

B9 An exhibition of fantastic firsts

CD 109

a) Listen to the CD and number the pictures in the right order.

how to listen TB p.143

b) Listen again. What is special about the inventions? Take notes.

c) ☾ Which is your favourite invention? Describe it and say why you like it.

☼ Describe two inventions in detail. Write about them in your exercise book.

B10 A ride in an amphicar

Reporter Ben Sickness is interviewing Karen Waterman about a special car. Read the questions. Then listen and answer ...

CD 110

- ☆ **two questions. You can choose.**
- ☾ **four questions. You can choose.**
- ☼ **all the questions.**

1. What is the weekly report on Radio 12 called? ______________________
2. What is Karen's job? ______________________
3. Why is the car called Amphicar? ______________________
4. How fast can the Amphicar go? ______________________
5. How do you steer the Amphicar? ______________________
6. What is the noise at the end? ______________________

Tipp
kilometres per hour = kph

B11 A solar marshmallow cooker

a) Look at the text and the pictures. What kind of text is it? Tick the correct answer.

☐ a story ☐ instructions ☐ an article

model text

You need: a cardboard box, aluminium foil, some flexible and some stiff cardboard, some tape, a wooden stick, marshmallows

1. Draw curves on the long sides of the cardboard box as in the picture. The sides have to be symmetrical. Cut out the curves.
2. Cut out a piece of flexible cardboard. Stick aluminium foil on the cardboard with the shiny side out. Do not wrinkle the foil!
3. Fix the cardboard on the opening of the box with some tape. Start at the centre.
4. Stick two pieces of stiff cardboard to each side of the box as holders.
5. Put marshmallows on a stick. Then put the stick through the holders.

Use your marshmallow cooker in sunny weather around lunchtime. You'll always have a nice dessert!

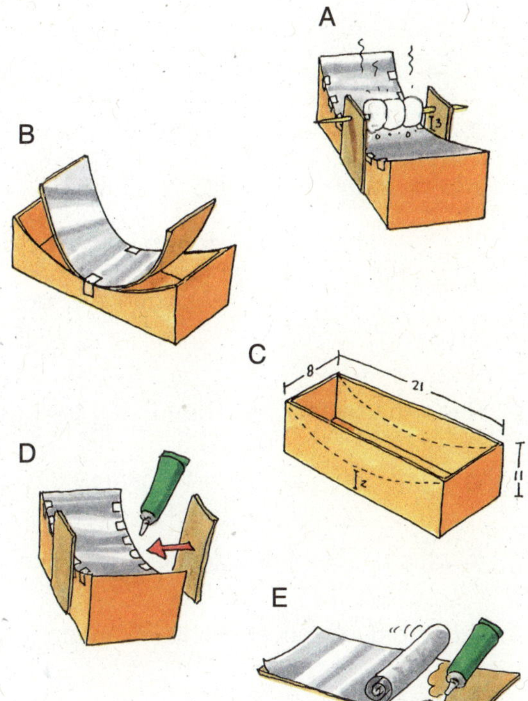

b) Match the parts of the text with the pictures.

1 ☐ 2 ☐ 3 ☐ 4 ☐ 5 ☐

c) Work with a partner. Explain in German how to make a solar marshmallow cooker.

how to mediate TB p. 145

Auf Seite 21 kannst du noch einmal nachlesen, wie du mit den *Test-yourself*-Seiten arbeitest. Die Lösungen findest du ab Seite 127.

T1 Listening: Who invented it?

CD 116

☆ **a) Listen to a radio programme. What is it about?**

☐ the invention of the television ☐ the invention of the telephone ☐ Italian inventions

b) Read the questions. Then listen again and tick the right answers.

1. When did Antonio Meucci show his invention for the first time?
   - ☐ in 1802
   - ☐ in 1860
   - ☐ in 1916
2. Why wasn't he able to apply for a patent?
   - ☐ No one believed he was the inventor.
   - ☐ He died before he could apply.
   - ☐ He didn't have 200 dollars.

von 6

CD 116

☾ **a) Listen to a radio programme. What is it about?**

☐ the invention of the television ☐ the invention of the telephone ☐ Italian inventions

b) Read the questions. Then listen again and tick the right answers.

1. Where did Antonio Meucci and Alexander Graham Bell live?
   - ☐ in Italy
   - ☐ in Britain
   - ☐ in the United States
2. When did Meucci show his invention for the first time?
   - ☐ in 1802
   - ☐ in 1860
   - ☐ in 1916
3. What did Meucci use his invention for?
   - ☐ to talk to his wife at home
   - ☐ to talk to his workers in his factory
   - ☐ to talk to his wife when she was not at home
4. Why wasn't he able to apply for a patent?
   - ☐ No one believed he was the inventor.
   - ☐ He died before he could apply.
   - ☐ He didn't have 200 dollars.

von 10

CD 116

☼ **Read the questions. Then listen to a radio programme and note down the answers.**

Tipp
Du kannst die Radiosendung zweimal anhören.

1. What did Antonio Meucci invent? ______________________________
2. In which country did Meucci and Alexander Graham Bell live? ______________________________
3. When did Meucci show his invention for the first time? ______________________________
4. Why did he do experiments with electricity? ______________________________
5. Where did he use his invention? ______________________________
   ____
6. Why wasn't Meucci able to apply for a patent? ______________________________

von 12

T2 Reading: How crisps became popular

Read the text.

George Crum, an American cook, is often called the 'inventor' of crisps, but he did not really invent them. In the early 19th century you could already buy cookbooks with recipes for crisps in the USA. However, George played an important role in making them even more popular in the USA some time later. There are two different stories about how this started.
The first story goes like this: In 1853 George worked as a cook at a restaurant in Saratoga Springs. One day a guest complained[1] that his chips were too thick. George made thinner ones, but the customer did not like them either. So George finally fried potato slices[2] that were too thin to eat with a fork and put some extra salt on them. He hoped to annoy[3] the customer. However, the man was happy with them.
In the other story George's sister Wicks, who also worked at the restaurant, created crisps by accident. She cut off a small piece of potato which fell into a frying pan.[4] Her brother tasted it, liked it and said: "We'll have plenty of those."
A few years later George opened his own restaurant, which became famous for its fantastic food. People said that he always put a basket of crisps on every table.

[1] complain – *sich beklagen;* [2] slice – *Scheibe;* [3] annoy – *ärgern;* [4] frying pan – *Bratpfanne*

☆ **Answer the questions.**

1. When does the first story take place? ____________________
2. Why did the customer in the first story complain? ____________________
3. Who created crisps in the first story? ____________________
4. Who created crisps in the second story? ____________________

von 8

☾ **Tick right or wrong.**

	right	wrong
1. George Crum wrote bestselling cookbooks.	☐	☐
2. In the first story a guest didn't like his chips, but loved his crisps.	☐	☐
3. George wanted to be nice to the customer.	☐	☐
4. In the second story crisps were created by George's brother.	☐	☐
5. Later George had his own restaurant and always put crisps on the tables.	☐	☐

von 10

☼ **Tick right or wrong.**

	right	wrong
1. Americans didn't know crisps before 1853.	☐	☐
2. The text doesn't say which story about George Crum is true.	☐	☐
3. The first story takes place in George's own restaurant in Saratoga Springs.	☐	☐
4. The guest was first served thick chips, then thinner chips and then crisps.	☐	☐
5. In the second story crisps were created by George's brother.	☐	☐
6. They were created by accident but George decided to serve more of them.	☐	☐

von 12

Tipp
Mach eine Aufnahme oder sprich vor der Klasse.

T3 Speaking: Useful inventions for you

von 8

☆ Talk about an invention that you often use (a mobile phone, a computer, a bike, ...).

- What is it?
- What do you use it for?
- How often do you use it?
- Why do you like it?

You can start like this:

I often use ...
I need it to ...

von 12

☾ Talk about an invention that you often use (a mobile phone, a computer, a bike, ...).

- What is it?
- What do you use it for?
- Where and when do you use it?
- How often do you use it?
- What is special about it?
- Why do you like it?

von 16

☼ Talk about two inventions that you often use (a mobile phone, a computer, a bike, ...).

- What are they?
- What do you use them for?
- Where and when do you use them?
- What is special about them?

First talk about one invention and then about the other.

T4 Writing: Things that need electricity

Write about electricity.

- List some things at home and at school that need electricity to work.
- Describe two or more of the things in detail. What do you use them for?
- What do you have to do if you don't have these things?

☆ Write five sentences. ☾ Write eight sentences. ☼ Write ten sentences.

A lot of things at home and at school need electricity to work.

von 10

von 16

von 20

T5 Mediation: Josephine Cochrane

CD 117

Listen to some facts about Josephine Cochrane. Then answer ...

☆ **three questions in German. You can choose.**
☾ **five questions in German. You can choose.**
☼ **all the questions in German.**

1. Was hat Josephine Cochrane erfunden? ______
2. Welche Nationalität hatte sie? ______
3. Was war der Grund für ihre Erfindung? ______
______
______
______
4. In welchem Jahr erhielt sie ein Patent? ______
5. Wer waren die ersten Käufer? ______
6. Was geschah 1893? ______
7. Wann eröffnete Josephine Cochrane eine eigene Fabrik? ______

von 6

von 10

von 14

Trage die Punkte, die du erreicht hast, in diese Tabelle ein. Achte darauf, wie die Aufgabe gekennzeichnet ist (Stern, Mond oder Sonne). Insgesamt trägst du fünf Ergebnisse ein.

	☆	☾	☼
Listening	____ von 6	____ von 10	____ von 12
Reading	____ von 8	____ von 10	____ von 12
Speaking	____ von 8	____ von 12	____ von 16
Writing	____ von 10	____ von 16	____ von 20
Mediation	____ von 6	____ von 10	____ von 14

Mithilfe dieser Übersichten findest du heraus, wie du bei den einzelnen Aufgaben abgeschnitten hast. Markiere die Felder, die auf dich zutreffen.

	☆			☾			☼		
	Super!	Gut!	Nur Mut!	Super!	Gut!	Nur Mut!	Super!	Gut!	Nur Mut!
Listening	6–5	4–3	2–0	10–7	6–4	3–0	12–9	8–5	4–0
Reading	8–6	5–3	2–0	10–7	6–4	3–0	12–9	8–5	4–0
Speaking	8–6	5–3	2–0	12–9	8–5	4–0	16–12	11–6	5–0
Writing	10–7	6–4	3–0	16–12	11–6	5–0	20–14	13–8	7–0
Mediation	6–5	4–3	2–0	10–7	6–4	3–0	14–11	10–6	5–0

M1 Listening: Important inventions

CD 118

a) Listen to Jake and his grandma talking about inventions. Tick the inventions they mention.

- [ ] the coffee machine
- [ ] the dishwasher
- [ ] computers
- [ ] tablets
- [ ] mobile phones
- [ ] motorbikes
- [ ] cars
- [ ] trains
- [ ] planes
- [ ] television
- [ ] the watch
- [ ] the washing machine
- [ ] the oven
- [ ] the microwave

b) Read the sentences. Then listen again and tick the right answer.

Jake's grandma says that her own grandma …

- [ ] had to wash lots of dishes every day because she didn't have a dishwasher.
- [ ] had to cook food in a big pot on a fire because she didn't have an oven.
- [ ] had to wash all the dirty clothes by hand because she didn't have a washing machine.

M2 Reading: Simple but clever

Read about young inventor Chris Haas. Then tick the correct sentences.

In 1994, Chris Haas was just nine years old when he came up with a great invention for basketball training. Chris was a big basketball fan and liked to play with other kids. He noticed that his friends sometimes missed really easy shots because they didn't know how to hold the basketball. So he designed a special basketball with hands painted on which shows players where their hands have to be.
Chris first presented his invention at a competiton at his school. He didn't win, but his teachers liked the idea and told him that he should get a patent.
Chris did just that and started selling his basketball around the world. Today, lots of kids use it to learn how to play. It is sold in sports shops all over the world. Chris has earned a lot of money from his successful invention.

1. Chris invented his special basketball when he was nineteen years old. ☐
2. He invented it because he always missed shots when he played with his friends. ☐
3. It is a basketball with hands painted on. ☐
4. The basketball is great for training because players can see where to put their hands. ☐
5. Chris first presented the basketball during a sports lesson at his school. ☐
6. Chris didn't get a patent, but he has sold his invention successfully anyway. ☐
7. Today you can buy the basketball in different countries. ☐
8. Chris has become rich. ☐

M3 Grammar: Facts about mobile phones

Complete the sentences.

is • are • was • were

1. The first mobile call ___________ made by Martin Cooper, an American inventor, in 1973.
2. Cooper ___________ considered the 'father' of the mobile phone.
3. In 1984 the first mobile phones ___________ sold in the USA for about $4,000 each.
4. Voicemail ___________ added to mobile phones in 1986.
5. Today 70 % of mobile phones ___________ produced in China.
6. Did you know that in Britain more than 100,000 mobiles ___________ dropped in toilets by accident every year?

LiF p. 136 14

M4 Grammar: Young inventors

Complete the sentences.

awarded • eaten • invented • sold • supported • worn

1. Earmuffs, ice lollies and the Glo-Sheet were ______________________ by kids.
2. The three young inventors were all ______________________ patents.
3. Earmuffs are ______________________ when it it cold outside.
4. Millions of ice lollies are ______________________ in the USA every year.
5. Today the Glo-Sheet is also ______________________ on the Internet.
6. Nowadays young inventors are ______________________ by special organisations.

LiF p. 136 14

M5 Grammar: Useful products

Write these sentences in the passive.

1. Philo Farnsworth invented the television.

The television was invented by Philo Farnsworth.

2. Karl Benz designed the first car.

The first car ______________________

3. Billions of people around the world use computers.

Computers ______________________

4. Companies in Asia produce a lot of technical equipment.

____

LiF p. 136 14

D1 A short alphabet of inventions

Look through Theme 5 again. Find inventions starting with these letters.

A	________________	L	________________
B	________________	M	________________
C	________________	O	________________
D	________________	S	________________
E	________________	T	________________
H	________________	V	________________
I	________________	W	________________
K	________________	Z	________________

D2 Who?

Find the answers in the theme.

1. Who was awarded a patent in 1974? ________________
2. Who had to tidy his room yesterday? ________________
3. Who recommends visiting the Textiles Gallery at MOSI? ________________
4. Who invented X-ray glasses? ________________
5. Who took a photo in front of MOSI? ________________

D3 Difficult words

a) Write down the ten words in the theme that you find the most difficult.

________ ________ ________ ________ ________

________ ________ ________ ________ ________

b) Spell your words and your partner writes them down. Then check his or her spelling.

D4 A limerick

Read the limerick and learn it by heart.

There was a young lady called Joan
Who was really sad on her own.
Her mother bought Joan
A new mobile phone.
With that now Joan's never alone.

A1 My favourite music

a) Listen to Hassan talking about music and take notes.

CD 119

Hassan's favourite music	
Where he listens to it	
How he listens to it	
How it makes him feel	

b) Talk to a partner about **your** favourite music. Where and how do you listen to it? How does it make you feel?

A2 Sabrina's concert

☆ Look at TB A2 again. Then close your textbook and match the sentence parts. Draw lines.

The Gatecrashers	calls the number on the Gatecrashers' website.
The manager	have exams at school next week.
Sabrina and Mike	work as roadies for the Gatecrashers.
Gillian	are recording a new album next month.
Gillian and David	has booked the Electric Theatre for a gig.

☾ Look at TB A2 again. Then close your textbook and match the sentence parts.

1	The Gatecrashers have just come back	A	for a gig next weekend.	1	
2	The band are recording a new album	B	David's favourite band.	2	
3	The manager has booked the Electric Theatre	C	have already gone home.	3	
4	The Gatecrashers can have	D	a lot of stuff.	4	
5	Half of their roadies	E	from a very successful concert.	5	
6	They need roadies to help	F	before the concert.	6	
7	The Gatecrashers are not	G	four days off after the concert.	7	
8	Gillian and David have to carry	H	next month.	8	

☼ Look at TB A2 again and answer the questions in your exercise book.

1. How do you know that the Gatecrashers are a popular band? Give reasons from the text.
2. Why has the manager booked the Electric Theatre for a gig?
3. Why does Sabrina get angry with the manager?
4. When can the band get a rest and for how long?
5. Half of the roadies have gone home. What's the manager's idea?
6. What do the new roadies get for their work? Do you think that is fair?

A3 Rock show words

> Tipp
> Ihr könnt die Wortliste auf Seite 246–247 im TB zu Hilfe nehmen.

a • e • i • o • u

a) Complete the words with the missing vowels.

pr_t_ct   g_ _r   s_ght   _mpr_ss_v_   b_ckst_g_

s_cr_t   d_m_g_   t_chn_c_ _ns   r_sp_ns_bl_   s_ _nd syst_m

CD 122

b) Listen to the CD and check your words.

c) Read the sentences and fill in the words from a).

1. A band's ____________ consists of instruments, lights, speakers and many other things.
2. A ____________ makes live music louder.
3. A manager is ____________ for planning all the details of a band's tours.
4. Security guards ____________ bands and their instruments.
5. The music, sound and light ____________ are very busy before and during a concert.
6. Extremely loud music can ____________ your hearing.
7. Musicians that the audience can't see are ____________ band members.
8. These musicians play ____________ out of ____________.
9. Concerts with many sound and light effects are often really ____________.

A4 Verb + noun

a) Match the verbs with the nouns and phrases.

have • sing • play • record • set up • wear • protect • plan • carry • solve

people • earplugs • gear • an album • a song • a conversation • a stage • exams • a tour • a problem • instruments

> Tipp
> Oft ist mehr als eine Kombination möglich.

____________ ____________

____________ ____________

____________ ____________

____________ ____________

____________ ____________

b) Choose at least five combinations and write sentences with them in your exercise book.

A5 Tell us, Sabrina

a) After the concert Sabrina talks to some fans. They want to know lots of things about her. Match their questions with Sabrina's answers.

1 When do you get up in the morning?

2 Is it true that Mike is your boyfriend?

3 When is your birthday?

4 Do you do sport?

5 Can you cook?

6 Where do you want to live later?

A No, he isn't. He's just a good friend.

B Yes, I often jog in the park in the late afternoon.

C On a sunny island.

D I can make spaghetti with meat sauce.

E On weekdays I usually get up at 7 o'clock.

F It's on 5 July.

1	2	3	4	5	6

b) Listen to the CD and check. CD 123

c) Write down in your exercise book what Sabrina says. LiF p. 136 15

Sabrina tells the girl with the orange T-shirt that she …

She says that she …

A6 What do you think?

a) Ask your partner and tick his or her answers.

Do you think that …	yes	no
concert tickets are usually expensive?	☐	☐
the job of a tour manager is interesting?	☐	☐
going on a concert tour is good fun for bands?	☐	☐
it is bad for children and teenagers to become stars?	☐	☐
famous singers have a fantastic life?	☐	☐

b) Report to the class what your partner thinks. LiF p. 136 15

Juliane thinks that …

Ercan doesn't think that …

A7 Choose

1. Make a word web about music. Look at TB A1 to A3 again and use the wordbank on page 164 in your textbook.
2. Make a wordsearch with new words from TB A1 to A3 for your partner.
3. Write a diary entry for Sabrina the week after the concert when she is back at school.

A8 The perfect fan

a) This is a song Sabrina and the Gatecrashers often sing for their fans. Complete it.

Your /feɪs/ ____________ we've never /siːn/ ____________

To your /haʊs/ ____________ we've never /biːn/ ____________

But we /nəʊ/ ____________ you're out /ðeə/ ____________

And we really /laɪk/ ____________ you – yeah!

You're /wɪð/ ____________ us all the /taɪm/ ____________

You /lɑːf/ ____________, you /dɑːns/ ____________, you sing along

/kʌm/ ____________ and join us in our brand new /sɒŋ/ ____________

You send /ʌs/ ____________ letters, /'preznts/ ____________ and more

We've /'nevə/ ____________ felt like this /bɪ'fɔː/ ____________

You're the /'pɜːfɪkt/ ____________ fan – that's /truː/ ____________

So our /'mjuːsɪk/ ____________ is /dʒʌst/ ____________ for you.

CD 124

b) Listen to the song and check.

A9 Facts about Pink

a) Look at TB A4 again. Then tick the correct sentences.

1. Pink's real name is Alexa Bess More. ☐
2. She is American. ☐
3. She has got more than five tattoos. ☐
4. She is also an actress. ☐
5. She has won three Oscars. ☐
6. Her favourite colours are blue and pink. ☐
7. She doesn't eat meat. ☐

b) Compare your answers with a partner. Quote from the text.

Correct the wrong sentences in your exercise book.

A10 What Pink's fans say

a) Read the chat and find out what fans say about Pink. Use different colours to mark what they say about • her music • her ideas • her character • her looks.

Bullfrog	She's got a very powerful voice and she's simply fantastic on stage!
Cupcake	Pink has created her own style. Her hair, tattoos and clothes look so cool.
Dogbone	She knows what young people's lives are like. That's why I love her songs.
It's me!	I love animals and I love Pink because she is a big supporter of animal rights. What she does for animals is great.
Phoenix	Pink sings what she thinks, and she has got strong opinions. She is not afraid to speak her mind. Everything she sings is true.
StarStruck	I can't get enough of Pink's music and I also like her because she works for different charities and gives lots of money to them.
MissSerious	I haven't got a tattoo or pink hair but I just love her music! She has also helped me through some hard times with her songs. I want to thank her for going out there and being who she is. That's why I am who I am today.
Ally@home	I went to a Pink concert in Manchester a few months ago and I've been one of her greatest fans since then. Her music touches me deeply. She is also a nice person – open, friendly and very funny. Pink, you rock, babe!!!!

b) Draw a grid like this in your exercise book and take notes.

What fans like about Pink's …

music	character	ideas	looks
…	…	…	…

Do you think that Pink can be a role model[1] for young people? Say why or why not.

[1] role model – *Vorbild*

A11 Target task: A presentation on a concert

a) Listen to a German pupil giving a presentation on a concert and take notes. CD 126

1. When was the concert? ______________________
2. What kind of music was played? ______________________
3. Who played? ______________________
4. Where did the concert take place? ______________________
5. What was good? ______________________
6. What was not so good? ______________________

b) Listen again. Do you like the presentation? Why or why not? Talk to a partner.

B1 An art project

An English friend is visiting you. You suggest taking part in the art project that is described in this brochure. Tell your friend ...

- who can take part,
- where it is,
- when it is,
- how much it costs,
- what you can do there,
- what you would like to do there,
- what you have to do if you want to take part.

how to mediate TB p. 145

Kunstwoche für Jugendliche

Sichert euch schon jetzt einen Platz in der Jugendkunstwoche zu Beginn der Sommerferien! Gemeinsam mit anderen Teenagern könnt ihr in der Holzwerkstatt sägen und bauen oder im Malatelier eure fantasievollen Ideen auf Papier und Leinwand bringen. Wer lieber mit Medien arbeitet, kann ein Live-Hörspiel aufnehmen oder im Computerstudio kreativ sein. Im Tanzsaal wiederum stehen Freude an der Bewegung und Rhythmusgefühl im Vordergrund.

Ist etwas für euch dabei? Dann meldet euch schnell an!

Altersgruppe: 12 bis 15 Jahre
Kosten: frei

Termin: 14. bis 18. Juli
Täglich von 10 bis 17 Uhr
Mittagessen inklusive

Kunstinitiative im Jugendzentrum
Brückenstraße 24
Telefon: 02797/294157

Anmeldeformular herunterladen (PDF)

B2 Talking about art

a) Unscramble the sentences.

1. painting • an • This • unusual • is • piece of art • .

____

LiF p. 135 12

2. 2014 • created • artist • in • The • it • .

____

3. colours • purple • dominant • The • and pink • are • .

____

4. is • done • it • It • was • how • interesting • .

____

5. surprising • a • I • it • effect • has • think • .

____

CD 133

b) Listen to the CD and check your sentences.

CD 2/22 134

c) Read these sentences. Then listen to the audio guide in TB B3 again. The artist talks about his piece of art, which is an assemblage[1]. Tick what he says.

I believe we make ourselves by the objects we use, but we don't know we do this. ☐

Modern people need too many things. ☐

We use things so often that we don't even see them any more. ☐

Of course nobody looks carefully at the things they use. ☐

If we don't look at a thing consciously[2], the thing isn't really there. ☐

This assemblage was very difficult to make. ☐

d) Start a poster together. Make a list of useful phrases for talking about art. Put it up in your classroom and add more phrases to it when you talk about different works of art.

[1]assemblage – *Assemblage (dreidimensionaler Gegenstand, der aus einer Kombination verschiedener Objekte entstanden ist)*; [2]consciously – *bewusst*

B3 Your ideas about a painting

a) Look at this painting. What can you see? What do you think is interesting, unusual, strange, …? Note down your ideas.

____

____

____

____

____

____

b) Talk about the painting in groups of three or four. Take notes about your classmates' ideas.

name	ideas about the painting

c) Present some of your group's ideas to the class.

I think that …

Samira thinks that …

Ole doesn't think that …

LiF p. 136 15

B4 Another painting by Chagall

a) Use these phrases to describe the painting by Marc Chagall:

in the centre • in the background • in the foreground • on the right • on the left • at the top • at the bottom

Tipp
Schlage neue Wörter nach.

b) Think of a title for the picture.

c) Compare your titles in class.

B5 Words to describe art

a) You have to know different adjectives to describe pieces of art really well. Make a table in your exercise book. Then sort the adjectives from the box into the lists. You can fill in many adjectives more than once.

beautiful • black • boring • bright • cold • colourful • dangerous • dark • depressing • dreamlike • funny • happy • interesting • realistic • sad • scary • strange • ugly • unusual • warm

Describing pieces of art: adjectives for ...

colours	people	things	the atmosphere	my own opinion
bright	...	...	...	...

wordbank art TB p. 165

b) Find more adjectives and add them to your lists. You can use a dictionary.

c) Choose at least eight adjectives and find nouns that go with them.

bright sky, sad clown, interesting objects, ...

d) Compare your lists and your adjective-noun combinations in class.

B6 Famous pieces of art

a) You can find all these pieces of art in Theme 6 in your textbook. Choose your favourite one and tick it.

☐ L. S. Lowry, *Coming out of School* (1927)

☐ Marc Chagall, *The Blue Circus* (1950)

☐ Malcolm Morley, *Mariner* (1998)

☐ Pablo Picasso, *Goat* (1946)

☐ Henri Matisse, *The Snail* (1953)

☐ René Magritte, *Empire of light* (1953/54)

b) Listen to the audio guide for your work of art. Take notes in the grid.

CD 135 136 137 138 139 140

Title	
Artist's name	
Information about the artist	
Information about the piece of art	

c) Work in a group of pupils who have listened to the same audio guide. Compare your notes.

d) Now get together in a group of pupils who have all listened to different audio guides. Inform each other about your pictures.

e) With your second group, give a talk about different works of art. Present one piece of art each.

Auf Seite 21 kannst du noch einmal nachlesen, wie du mit den *Test-yourself*-Seiten arbeitest. Die Lösungen findest du ab Seite 128.

T1 Listening: Roadie – a cool job?

CD 145

Ishaq and Angus meet Yasir, who works as a roadie. Listen to the dialogue. What do roadies do in their job? Tick the tasks Yasir talks about.

Tipp
Du kannst den Dialog zweimal anhören.

1. Roadies sell concert tickets. ☐
2. They lift and carry heavy equipment. ☐
3. They work at mixing desks and control the sound. ☐
4. They put up sound systems. ☐
5. They put up video equipment. ☐
6. They make videos of the concerts. ☐
7. They fix lighting. ☐
8. Some roadies drive the trucks and the tour buses. ☐

von 8

CD 145

Ishaq and Angus meet Yasir, who works as a roadie. Listen to the dialogue. What does Yasir say about his job? Complete the information.

1. Yasir has been on ________________ big tours this year.
2. During a tour roadies usually work ________________ a week.
3. Roadies put up ________________________ and ________________________.
4. They also fix ________________________.
5. Some roadies drive the trucks and the ________________________.
6. Ishaq and Angus are happy because Yasir can get them ________________________.

von 14

CD 145

Ishaq and Angus meet Yasir, who works as a roadie. Read the questions. Then listen to the dialogue and note down the answers.

1. What do roadies do in their job? (Write down five tasks.) ________________________

____

____

____

2. How many roadies do famous bands need? ________________________
3. Why are Ishaq and Angus happy at the end? ________________________

____

von 14

T2 Reading: Tate Modern

Read about Tate Modern.

Tate Modern is a famous art gallery in London and one of the largest museums of modern art in the world. It has a collection of British art from 1900 to the present day and also many pieces of international modern art. Tate Modern is open from 10 am to 6 pm from Sunday to Thursday and from 10 am to 10 pm on Friday and Saturday. As in all the other national galleries and museums in the United Kingdom, admission[1] to the collection is free. Visitors only have to buy tickets for special exhibitions. Disabled people then pay concessionary rates[2].

Tate Modern offers many activities for children and families. When you enter the museum you can take a free map, which makes it easy to find your way around. The museum staff encourage[3] young people to visit the museum. They think that you don't have to be an expert to talk about art. You can just enjoy looking at the pieces of art and take whatever you like from them.

Why don't you visit Tate online at kids.tate.org.uk? You can upload your own pieces of art, play games, watch videos about art and artists, find ideas for crafts[4] and send e-cards.

[1] admission – *Eintritt;* [2] concessionary rate – *verbilligter Preis;* [3] encourage – *ermutigen, ermuntern;* [4] crafts – *hier: Bastelarbeiten*

Cross out the wrong information.

1. Tate Modern has a collection of **British and international art/of British and Indian art**.
2. The gallery opens at **6 o'clock/10 o'clock** in the morning.
3. On Saturdays you can stay in the gallery until **8 o'clock/10 o'clock** in the evening.
4. You can also visit Tate online at **www.kids-at-tate.uk/kids.tate.org.uk**.

von 8

Tick right or wrong.

	right	wrong
1. Tate Modern is a very famous, but quite small art gallery in London.	☐	☐
2. You can see modern British art and modern international art at the gallery.	☐	☐
3. The museum opens at 10 o'clock in the morning every day.	☐	☐
4. On Sundays you can stay in the museum until 10 o'clock at night.	☐	☐
5. Admission is free, but not to special exhibitions.	☐	☐
6. You should know a lot about modern art if you want to visit the museum.	☐	☐

von 12

Tick yes or no.

	yes	no
1. Can you see 19th-century art at Tate Modern?	☐	☐
2. Can you see art from different countries at the gallery?	☐	☐
3. Is it possible to stay at the gallery until 10 pm on Thursdays?	☐	☐
4. Do you have to pay to see the collection?	☐	☐
5. Do disabled people have to pay to see special exhibitions?	☐	☐
6. Should you know a lot about modern art if you want to visit the museum?	☐	☐
7. Can you see pictures by other kids on the website of the gallery?	☐	☐

von 14

T3 Speaking: A painting

Tipp
Mach eine Aufnahme oder sprich vor der Klasse.

Describe the painting by Vincent van Gogh. You can make some notes before you talk.

- What can you see?
- Where are the things?
- What colour are they?
- Who do you think lives in the room – a child, a man or a woman? Give reasons.
- What do you think is interesting or unusual about the painting?
- Do you like it? Why or why not?

☆ Talk for about one minute.
☾ Talk for about 1.5 minutes.
☼ Talk for about two minutes.

von 10
von 16
von 20

T4 Writing: Your favourite music

Write about your favourite music OR your favourite singer OR your favourite band.

- What is special about the music?
- Where and when do you listen to it?
- What do you know about the singer or the band?
- How many of their songs do you know or have you got?
- How does the music make you feel?

☆ Write five sentences. ☾ Write eight sentences. ☼ Write ten sentences.

Tipp
Du kannst auch über verschiedene Musikrichtungen, zwei Sänger oder Sängerinnen oder zwei Bands schreiben.

von 10
von 16
von 20

T5 Mediation: A workshop

Read the advert from a website with tips for teenagers on great things to do in London.

☆ **Answer three questions in German.**
☾ **Answer five questions in German.**
☼ **Answer all the questions in German.**

1. Worum geht es in der Anzeige?

2. Wer macht das Angebot?

3. Wer kann teilnehmen?

4. Wann findet das Angebot statt?

5. Was kostet es?

6. Wie kann man es buchen?

Graffiti & Street Art Workshop

Jason, a professional London graffiti artist, will show you his techniques and help you create your own piece of art. The workshop will introduce you to the use of spray paints and other graffiti art materials. The equipment for the day will be provided. Don't miss it – book now!

Suitable for kids from 8 to 16
Parents and other adults welcome

Every Saturday and Sunday
from 11 am to 3 pm

Jason Lacombe, Hanbury Street, London
(Exact address will be given after booking)

Choose date

Kids £20 | Adults £35

Book now

von 6

von 10

von 12

Trage deine Punkte in diese Tabelle ein. Es sind insgesamt fünf Ergebnisse.

	☆	☾	☼
Listening	____ von 8	____ von 14	____ von 14
Reading	____ von 8	____ von 12	____ von 14
Speaking	____ von 10	____ von 16	____ von 20
Writing	____ von 10	____ von 16	____ von 20
Mediation	____ von 6	____ von 10	____ von 12

Finde heraus, wie du abgeschnitten hast. Markiere die Felder, die auf dich zutreffen.

	☆			☾			☼		
	Super!	Gut!	Nur Mut!	Super!	Gut!	Nur Mut!	Super!	Gut!	Nur Mut!
Listening	8–6	5–3	2–0	14–11	10–6	5–0	14–11	10–6	5–0
Reading	8–6	5–3	2–0	12–9	8–5	4–0	14–11	10–6	5–0
Speaking	10–7	6–4	3–0	16–12	11–6	5–0	20–14	13–8	7–0
Writing	10–7	6–4	3–0	16–12	11–6	5–0	20–14	13–8	7–0
Mediation	6–5	4–3	2–0	10–7	6–4	3–0	12–9	8–5	4–0

M1 Listening: After the Gatecrashers' concert

CD 146

Listen to Sabrina and her manager talking about the concert at the Electric Theatre and tick the right information.

1. The Gatecrashers made …
   - about £150. ☐
   - about £1,000. ☐
   - about £1,500. ☐
2. The manager was pleased with …
   - the secret band members. ☐
   - the new helpers. ☐
   - the new music technicians. ☐
3. The manager hired …
   - 15 roadies. ☐
   - 40 roadies. ☐
   - 50 roadies. ☐
4. The next rehearsal is …
   - on Tuesday. ☐
   - on Friday. ☐
   - on Saturday. ☐

M2 Reading: Is it real?

Read about a piece of art. Then tick right or wrong.

From a distance you see a young man lying on the ground. He is wearing jeans and a blue shirt. He has taken off his shoes and is lying on his back with a little white pillow under his head. His legs are bent.
As soon as you get closer, you will find that he is taller than a real person. And you will realise that he is not breathing. He is a painted sculpture[1], but painted so well that you think he is real.
British artist Sean Henry, who created the sculpture in 2004 and called it *Catafalque*, says it has an important message: the man is thinking about our place in the universe[2]. He is trying to understand why we are here and what we are doing. "These are thoughts that have always been with me, all the time", says Sean Henry, who actually looks a bit like his sculpture.

[1] sculpture – *Skulptur;* [2] universe – *Universum*

	right	wrong
1. The sculpture was created by an American artist.	☐	☐
2. The artist's name is Sean Henry.	☐	☐
3. The artist looks a bit like the sculptured man.	☐	☐
4. The sculpture was created in 2014.	☐	☐
5. It has the title *Catastrophe*.	☐	☐
6. The sculptured man is as tall as a real person.	☐	☐
7. He isn't wearing shoes.	☐	☐
8. He is trying to understand why he has to lie in a park.	☐	☐

M3 Words: Useful adjectives

a) Complete the adjectives with the endings in the box.

-able • -al • -ant • -ing • -ible • -ive

relev__________ impress__________ respons__________

amaz__________ reli__________ profession__________

b) Which word from a) is the same as a noun?

____

c) Choose adjectives from a) to complete the sentences.

1. If you say that a concert is ______________________ you think that it is fantastic.
2. A person who dances as a job is a ______________________ dancer.
3. Facts that you have to know to do a task are ______________________ information.
4. If your friends never lie to you or talk behind your back, they are ______________________.

M4 Grammar: Opinions about Sabrina

a) Read what some people say about Sabrina.

b) Write down what the people say.

Arabella says that ______________________________

____

____

____

LiF p. 136
15

D1 Where are they?

Look through Theme 6 again and find these people, animals and things.

1. There is a big yellow flower on page ____________.
2. There is a girl in a white T-shirt on page ____________.
3. There is a Chinese text on page ____________.
4. There is a man with a blue tie on page ____________.
5. There are three bottles of water on page ____________.
6. There is a school building on page ____________.

D2 Who or what is it?

Find the answers in the theme.

1. Who controls what the audience hears at a concert? ____________.
2. Who said that everyone is an artist? ____________.
3. Who thinks that music can change the world? ____________.
4. What is the app of Tate Modern called? ____________.

D3 A word quiz

How many words can you find in 'professional musician'?

____

____

D4 People and things

Complete the words.

1. A person who shows you pieces of art in a museum: g □ □ □ □
2. A picture on a canvas: p □ □ □ □ □ □ □
3. The people in your family: □ □ l □ □ □ □ □ □
4. A private talk between people: □ □ n □ □ □ s □ □ □ □ □
5. What someone else has said: □ □ o □ □ t □ □ □

Vergleiche deine Antworten zu den Aufgaben in *Test yourself* mit den Lösungen. Zähle und notiere deine Punkte. Trage sie in die Kästchen in den Randspalten auf den *Test-yourself*-Seiten und anschließend in die Tabellen am Ende jedes *Test-yourself*-Teils ein. Berechne dann deine Gesamtpunktzahl und befasse dich in Ruhe mit den Auswertungen, die du ebenfalls in den Tabellen am Ende von *Test yourself* findest.

Theme 1: Eating out

T1 Listening: Are you ready to order?

a) a curry house a Japanese restaurant
b) Scene 1: chicken curry vegetable masala
Scene 2: sushi spicy fish on crispy rice

a) a curry house a Japanese restaurant a pub
b) Scene 1: chicken curry vegetable masala
Scene 2: sushi spicy fish on crispy rice
Scene 3: cheeseburger small salad

a) a curry house a Japanese restaurant a pub an Italian restaurant
b) Scene 1: chicken curry vegetable masala
Scene 2: sushi spicy fish on crispy rice
Scene 3: cheeseburger small salad
Scene 4: beef lasagna spaghetti carbonara olives
(Auch wenn du die Namen der Gerichte etwas falsch geschrieben hast, erhältst du die volle Punktzahl.)

Für jede richtige Lösung erhältst du zwei Punkte.

von 12 von 18 von 26

T2 Reading: Eating habits in Great Britain

1. right 2. wrong 3. wrong 4. right

1. wrong 2. wrong 3. right 4. wrong 5. wrong

1. It is food that people take to school or to work for lunch (in a plastic box, often a sandwich, a small bag of crisps, a piece of fruit and a drink).
2. 'tea', 'dinner' or 'supper'
3. two vegetables
4. a dish of meat (beef, lamb or pork) that you eat with gravy, vegetables, potatoes and Yorkshire pudding
5. *zwei dieser Antworten:* be impolite, not say "thank you" when they serve you something, start eating before the others, talk with food in your mouth

Für jede richtige Lösung erhältst du zwei Punkte.

von 8 von 10 von 10

T3 Speaking: Ordering food

Partner/in A: Kellner/Kellnerin	Partner/in B: Gast
1 Hello./Good evening. Are you ready to order?	**2** Yes, I'd like …, please.
3 And what would you like to drink?	**4** A/An …, please.
1 Hello./Good evening. Are you ready to order?	**2** Yes, I'd like …, please.
3 Would you like any side dishes?	**4** Yes, some olives/some bread/…, please.
5 And what would you like to drink?	**6** A/An …, please.
7 Here you are.	**8** Thank you. Can I have the bill, please?
9 I'll be with you in a minute. That's … pounds.	**10** Here you are.
11 Thank you. Have a nice evening.	**12** Thank you. You too.

Für jede korrekt formulierte Frage und Antwort erhältst du zwei Punkte.

von 4 von 6 von 12

T4 Writing: Your favourite food

Lösungsbeispiel:
My favourite food is lasagna. It is an Italian dish. I like it because there is a lot of meat sauce and cheese in it. My mum often makes it for me at the weekend. I sometimes eat it in an Italian restaurant, too. Another dish I really like is *schnitzel* with potatoes and salad. My grandma makes the best *schnitzels*. She often makes them for me when I visit her. I always put lots of lemon juice on the meat. That is really delicious.

Für jeden korrekt formulierten Satz erhältst du zwei Punkte. Zeige deinen Text einer Person, die gut Englisch spricht.

☆ ___ von 10 ☾ ___ von 16 ☼ ___ von 20

T5 Mediation: At Pizza World

1. *Die billigste große Pizza kostet £7.75 (Ciao Bambino), die teuerste kostet £12.95 (Verde).*
2. *Ja*
3. *Ja, Ciao Bambino, Mexicana und Verde*
4. *Ja, den Salat mit Hühnchen*
5. *£16.30*

Für jede richtige Antwort erhältst du zwei Punkte.

☆ ___ von 4 ☾ ___ von 6 ☼ ___ von 10

Theme 2: On the street

T1 Listening: Being a lion kid

☆ 1. 11 2. young Simba 3. 14 weeks 4. twice a week

☾ 1. 11 2. young Simba 3. his grandmother 4. 14 weeks 5. nothing 6. twice a week

☼ 1. young Simba 2. at a theatre school for kids 3. a training programme for young kids who want to be in 'The Lion King' 4. 14 weeks 5. *zwei der folgenden Gründe:* Simba is a wonderful character. / Simba is brave and athletic. / Simba is a real hero. It is great to play a hero. / Some scenes with Timon and Pumba are lots of fun. 6. twice a week

Für jede richtige Lösung erhältst du zwei Punkte.

☆ ___ von 8 ☾ ___ von 12 ☼ ___ von 14

T2 Reading: A success story

☆ 1B 2D 3A 4C

☾ 1. wrong 2. wrong 3. right 4. wrong 5. right

☼ 1. three 2. Minneapolis 3. stilts 4. *zwei dieser Antworten:* London, Paris, Hamburg 5. 2030 6. 32

Für jede richtige Lösung erhältst du zwei Punkte.

☆ ___ von 8 ☾ ___ von 10 ☼ ___ von 12

T3 Speaking: Buying trainers

Lösungsbeispiel:

☆ **Partner A (seller)**
1 Can I help you?
3 I've got a pair of black trainers. Look here. Do you want / Would you like to try them on?
5 They're £18.
7 Thank you. Goodbye. / Bye.

Partner B (customer)
2 I'm looking for trainers.
4 Yes, please. They fit. / They're perfect. How much are they?
6 I'll take them. Here you are.
8 Goodbye. / Bye.

Partner A (seller)
1 Hello, can I help you?
3 What size do you need?
5 I've got a pair of black trainers. Look here. Do you want to try them on?
7 They're £18.
9 Thank you. Goodbye./Bye.

Partner B (customer)
2 I'm looking for trainers.
4 I need a size …
6 Yes, please. They fit./They're perfect. How much are they?
8 That's a bargain. (I'll take them.) Here you are.
10 Goodbye./Bye.

1 Hello, can I help you?
3 What size do you need?
5 I've got a pair of black trainers. Look here. They're almost new. Do you want to try them on?
7 They're £18.
9 Thank you. Goodbye./Bye.

2 I'm looking for trainers.
4 I need a size …
6 Yes, please. I like them because they are really comfortable and they look great. How much are they?
8 That's a bargain./That's not expensive./That's a good price. (I'll take them.) Here you are.
10 Goodbye./Bye.

Für jeden korrekt formulierten Dialogteil erhältst du zwei Punkte.

☆ ___ von 8   ☾ ___ von 10   ☼ ___ von 10

T4 Writing: Events in your area

Lösungsbeispiel:
I love the funfairs in my hometown. They always take place at Wilhelmsplatz, a big square in the city centre. They take place twice a year, in spring and in autumn, and they always last a week. I go there with my friends, my parents or my cousins. I can't go very often because the rides are quite expensive. I try to save money for the funfairs. My favourite rides are the swing carousel and the rollercoaster. I also like the bumper cars. My friends and I like the food at the funfairs, too. You can buy sausages, candyfloss, toffee apples and roasted almonds.

Für jeden korrekt formulierten Satz erhältst du zwei Punkte. Zeige deinen Text einer Person, die gut Englisch spricht.

☆ ___ von 10   ☾ ___ von 16   ☼ ___ von 20

T5 Mediation: A car boot sale

1. *Auf dem Parkplatz in der Holloway Road*
2. *Am Samstag, dem 29. August*
3. *Er beginnt um 9 Uhr und endet um 16 Uhr.*
4. *Nichts./Der Eintritt ist frei.*
5. *Nichts (Es gibt nur Getränke.)*
6. *Man bezahlt £7 für einen Stellplatz, wenn man vorher bucht, und £10, wenn man einfach so erscheint.*
7. *Man kann unter der angegebenen Telefonnummer anrufen oder eine E-Mail schicken.*

Für jede richtige Antwort erhältst du zwei Punkte.

☆ ___ von 8   ☾ ___ von 10   ☼ ___ von 14

Theme 3: Be a sport

T1 Listening: Successful fundraising

☆ 1. a walk-a-thon 2. six 3. eight 4. last Saturday

☾ 1. a walk-a-thon 2. £18,000 3. 532 4. £43
5. gym equipment, the bathrooms in the gym, computers, the partner school in Africa

☼ 1. a walk-a-thon 2. £18,000 3. 532 4. 11 5. £25 6. £43 7. last Saturday
8. gym equipment, the bathrooms in the gym, computers, the partner school in Africa

Für jede richtige Lösung erhältst du zwei Punkte. ☆ ___ von 8 ☾ ___ von 16 ☼ ___ von 22

T2 Reading: Fastest runner ever

☆ 1. Jamaica 2. sprinting 3. three times 4. 9.58 seconds in the 100 metres

☾ *Folgende Sätze sind korrekt:*
3. He won three gold medals at three Olympic Games.
4. He has been very successful at some world championships, too.
5. Usain's personal best is also the fastest time any person has ever run.

☼ 1. in Jamaica 2. 94 kg 3. on 21 August 2016 4. in 2012 5. Because 'Bolt' is Usain's last name.

Für jede richtige Lösung erhältst du zwei Punkte. ☆ ___ von 8 ☾ ___ von 10 ☼ ___ von 10

T3 Speaking: In the waiting room

Beispiel für den Dialog:

Patient/in A:

☆☾☼
1 What's wrong with you?
3 Oh, that sounds bad/terrible.
5 I stepped on some broken glass and cut my foot.

☾☼
7 How did you break your arm?
9 Oh, too bad./Oh, how awful. The doctor will probably take an X-ray of your arm.

☼
11 Well, I hope the doctor will see us soon.
13 I've been waiting even longer. Oh, I can see the doctor now. Good luck and get well soon.

Patient/in B:

2 I think I've broken my arm.
4 Yes, it really hurts. And what's wrong with you?
6 That's bad/terrible, too.
8 I went inline skating in the park and fell.
10 I think so, too. I've never had an X-ray.
12 I hope so, too. I've been waiting for over an hour.
14 Thanks. I hope the doctor will help you, too. Bye.

Für jeden richtigen Dialogteil erhältst du zwei Punkte. ☆ ___ von 6 ☾ ___ von 10 ☼ ___ von 14

T4 Writing: Charlene's sport

☆☾☼ *Lösungsbeispiel:*
Charlene does gymnastics. She is very good at it. She has been a member of a girls' team for four years. She goes to training twice a week. Before competitions training takes place even more often. Charlene needs special clothes for her sport: leotards and gym shoes. Her favourite discipline is aerobic gymnastics. You do it in small groups and perform to music. Charlene has taken part in three competitions with her team in the last two years. Last time they won the first prize.

Für jeden korrekt formulierten Satz erhältst du zwei Punkte. Zeige deinen Text einer Person, die gut Englisch spricht. ☆ ___ von 10 ☾ ___ von 16 ☼ ___ von 20

T5 Mediation: Useful tips for bake sales

☾ ☼ *Es geht um einen Kuchenbasar/einen Kuchenverkauf zu Wohltätigkeitszwecken.*

Anschließend ist eine Auswahl folgender Antworten korrekt:

- *Man sollte die Kuchen und Plätzchen selbst backen und dafür einfache Rezepte auswählen, weil wenige Zutaten geringere Kosten bedeuten. Man kann auch Fertigbackmischungen für Kuchen und Brownies verwenden.*
- *Man sollte sich vor und nach dem Backen die Hände waschen.*
- *Man kann in eine Bäckerei gehen und sich dort die Preise für Kuchen ansehen. Man kann sich bei den Preisen auch von einem Erwachsenen beraten lassen.*
- *Man kann Preisschilder aus kleinen Zetteln anfertigen und diese vorn auf die Kuchenplatten stellen.*
- *Man kann einen Tisch als Stand herrichten. Am besten legt man eine hübsche Tischdecke darauf.*
- *Man sollte ein großes buntes Schild gestalten, um die Leute auf den Stand aufmerksam zu machen.*
- *Man sollte eine Kiste für das Geld haben, das man einnimmt. Man sollte vorher genügend Wechselgeld hineinlegen.*
- *Man sollte sehr freundlich zu den Kunden sein und ihnen Zeit zum Auswählen lassen.*

Für jede richtige Antwort erhältst du zwei Punkte. ☆ ___ von 6 ☾ ___ von 10 ☼ ___ von 16

Theme 4: No man is an island

T1 Listening: Stuart's worries

☆
a) He gets very nervous when he has to give a presentation.
b) "Sometimes I can't talk at all." "I could try it out."

☾
a) Stuart gets very nervous when he has to give a presentation.
b) Stuart can practise presentations with Ibrahim.
Stuart can ask Ibrahim to make a video when he is practising.

☼
a) He gets very nervous when he has to give a presentation.
b) Stuart can practise presentations with Ibrahim.
Stuart can ask Ibrahim to make a video when he is practising.
Stuart can learn his presentations by heart.

Für jede richtige Lösung erhältst du zwei Punkte. ☆ ___ von 6 ☾ ___ von 6 ☼ ___ von 8

T2 Reading: The real Robinson

☆ 1. in 1676 2. in 1721 3. for four years and four months 4. Robinson Crusoe Island

☾ 1. in Scotland. 2. *Cinque Ports.* 3. water and milk. 4. in 1711. 5. Robinson Crusoe Island.

☼
1. 28 years old
2. in the South Pacific (about 600 km west of Chile)
3. He ate wild vegetables and goat meat. He drank water and goat milk.
4. One for cooking and one for sleeping
5. Once he fell and couldn't move for a whole day. Two times he had to hide when Spanish ships came to the island.

Für jede richtige Lösung erhältst du zwei Punkte. ☆ ___ von 8 ☾ ___ von 10 ☼ ___ von 10

T3 Speaking: Problems between children and parents

Beispiele für Dialoge:

Mother: Oh no, Cleo. You're still on the phone. Can you please stop talking and help me around the house?
Daughter: Oh, Mum. I'm talking to Emma. It's important.
Mother: You see Emma at school every day. Why do you have to talk to her on the phone for hours now?
Daughter: Mum! I said it's important. Emma has got a problem.
Mother: Cleo, I asked you to clean the bathroom half an hour ago.
Daughter: I can do it later.
Mother: Well, I'm sorry but we want to go to Grandma's at twelve. Please clean the bathroom before we leave.
Daughter: Mum, I can still clean it when we get back tonight.
Mother: Cleo, we won't get back before nine or ten. It's too late then.
Daughter: OK, OK, I'll do it in ten minutes.
Mother: Alright. And please stop eating crisps. Grandma has made a nice lunch for us and you won't be hungry if you eat too much now.
Daughter: Oh, Mum!

Son: Bye, Dad, I'll be back around seven.
Father: Where are you going, Joseph?
Son: To the halfpipe. Greg is there, too.
Father: Have you finished your homework?
Son: No, not yet.
Father: Well, I'm sorry, Joseph, but you have to do your homework first. I know that you have a maths test on Friday. You have to practise for that.
Son: Oh, Dad, I'm good at maths. I don't have to practise.
Father: OK, if you think so. But you definitely have to do your homework before you can go out.
Son: It's not much, Dad. I can do it tonight. Now the sun is shining. And Greg is waiting for me.
Father: Call him and tell him you'll come later.
Son: That's so unfair, Dad. All the others can meet their friends in the afternoon.
Father: You can meet Greg, too, after you've done your homework. You'd better get started.

Für jeden richtigen Dialogteil erhältst du zwei Punkte.

☆ ___ von 8 ☾ ___ von 10 ☼ ___ von 12

T4 Writing: Josephine's day

Lösungsbeispiel:

Josephine gets up early and she only has a small breakfast. The hospital where she works is in Paddington. That is far away from Hendon. Josephine takes the underground to work. She buys a newspaper on the way to the station and reads it on the train. She is always very busy at work. On sunny days she has lunch in a park near the hospital. She loves her job although she is often tired. In the evening she helps her parents around the house. At the weekend she usually meets her boyfriend.

Für jeden richtigen Satz erhältst du zwei Punkte.

☆ ___ von 10 ☾ ___ von 16 ☼ ___ von 20

T5 Mediation: Holidays on the Isle of Wight

Eine Auswahl folgender Antworten ist korrekt:

- *zum Strand gehen und dort schwimmen*
- *die Küste entlang wandern*
- *auf der Insel wandern*
- *hübsche Dörfer (mit schönen alten Häusern) besichtigen*
- *Vögel beobachten/an einer Vogelbeobachtungstour teilnehmen*
- *einen Abenteuerpark besuchen*
- *ein Dinosauriermuseum besuchen*

Für jede richtige Antwort erhältst du zwei Punkte.

☆ ___ von 6 ☾ ___ von 8 ☼ ___ von 12

Theme 5: The world of science

T1 Listening: Who invented it?

☆ **a)** the invention of the telephone
b) 1. in 1860 2. He didn't have 200 dollars.

☾ **a)** the invention of the telephone
b) 1. in the United States 2. in 1860 3. to talk to his wife at home 4. He didn't have 200 dollars.

☼ 1. the telephone 2. the United States 3. in 1860 4. He wanted to help people with illnesses.
5. at home (His wife was ill and had to lie in bed. They could now talk when he was working downstairs.)
6. He didn't have 200 dollars.

Für jede richtige Lösung erhältst du zwei Punkte.

☆	☾	☼
von 6	von 10	von 12

T2 Reading: How crisps became popular

☆ 1. (At a restaurant) in Saratoga Springs 2. Because his chips were too thick 3. George (Crum)
4. George's sister Wicks

☾ 1. wrong 2. right 3. wrong 4. wrong 5. right

☼ 1. wrong 2. right 3. wrong 4. right 5. wrong 6. right

Für jede richtige Lösung erhältst du zwei Punkte.

☆	☾	☼
von 8	von 10	von 12

T3 Speaking: Useful inventions for you

Beispiele für Kurzvorträge:

☆ I often use my mobile phone. I need it to send messages to my friends, to listen to music, to play games and to use the Internet. I also take a lot of photos with it. I've got some really cool apps, for example … I use my mobile phone every day. I think it is very practical because you can chat with lots of people.

☾ ☼ I often use my mobile phone. I need it to send messages to my friends and classmates, to listen to music, to play games and to use the Internet. I also take a lot of photos with it. I really like editing photos – that's a lot of fun. I've got some really cool apps, for example … I use my mobile phone at home, on the way to school and when I go into town. I use it every day. I think it is very practical because you can chat with lots of people and stay in touch with your friends. We have a class chat and sometimes use it to help each other with our homework.

☼ I often use my computer, too. I only use it at home, usually in the afternoon or in the evening. I like playing computer games and watching music videos. I also need my computer to find information on the Internet. Sometimes I write texts for school on it. Last month we had to give a presentation in science so I used my computer to design a PowerPoint presentation.

Für jede richtig formulierte Aussage erhältst du zwei Punkte.

☆	☾	☼
von 8	von 12	von 16

T4 Writing: Things that need electricity

☆ ☾ ☼ *Lösungsbeispiel:*
A lot of things at home and at school need electricity to work. At home people often use toasters, kettles, electric ovens, hairdryers, lamps, TVs, radios, computers and mobile phone chargers. At school you need lamps, computers and whiteboards. A lot of people use their ovens almost every day. They need them to cook food. If you don't have an oven, you have to eat cold food like sandwiches or muesli or order food like pizza. People with long hair need a hairdryer to dry their hair. If they don't have one, they have to wait for a long time until their hair is dry. That is very unpractical when it is cold outside. Most families use their TVs to watch films, TV shows or the news, but if you don't have a TV, you can use your computer.

Für jeden richtigen Satz erhältst du zwei Punkte.

☆	☾	☼
von 10	von 16	von 20

T5 Mediation: Josephine Cochrane

1. *die Spülmaschine*
2. *Sie war Amerikanerin.*
3. *(Ihre Bediensteten zerbrachen beim Spülen oft Geschirr. Außerdem dauerte das Spülen immer sehr lange.) Sie wollte eine Maschine, die schnell spülte, ohne Geschirr zu zerbrechen.*
4. *1886*
5. *Hotels und Restaurants (in Chicago)*
6. *Cochrane gewann einen Preis für ihre Erfindung.*
7. *1897*

Für jede richtige Antwort erhältst du zwei Punkte. ☆ ___ von 6 ☾ ___ von 10 ☼ ___ von 14

Theme 6: Music and art

T1 Listening: Roadie – a cool job?

☆ *Folgende Aussagen sind korrekt:*

2. They lift and carry heavy equipment.
4. They put up sound systems.
5. They put up video equipment.
7. They fix lighting.
8. Some roadies drive the trucks and the tour buses.

☾
1. Yasir has been on <u>two</u> big tours this year.
2. During a tour roadies usually work <u>seven days</u> a week.
3. Roadies put up <u>sound systems</u> and <u>video equipment</u>.
4. They also fix <u>lighting</u>.
5. Some roadies drive the trucks and the <u>tour buses</u>.
6. Ishaq and Angus are happy because Yasir can get them <u>free (concert) tickets</u>.

☼
1. They lift and carry heavy equipment, put up sound systems, put up video equipment, fix lighting, drive the trucks and the tour buses. *(Wenn du* „put up sound systems and video equipment" *notiert hast, erhältst du dafür zusammen vier Punkte.)*
2. about 150
3. Yasir can get them free concert tickets/free tickets for a concert/free tickets for a Funky Four concert.

Für jede richtige Lösung erhältst du zwei Punkte. ☆ ___ von 8 ☾ ___ von 14 ☼ ___ von 14

T2 Reading: Tate Modern

☆ 1. of British and international art 2. 10 o'clock 3. 10 o'clock 4. kids.tate.org.uk

☾ 1. wrong 2. right 3. right 4. right 5. right 6. wrong

☼ 1. no 2. yes 3. no 4. no 5. yes 6. no 7. yes

Für jede richtige Lösung erhältst du zwei Punkte. ☆ ___ von 8 ☾ ___ von 12 ☼ ___ von 14

T3 Speaking: A painting

Beispiel für den Kurzvortrag:

You can see a bedroom in this picture. On the right there is a brown bed with a white pillow and a red duvet. There is a small brown and green chair next to the bed and another chair in front of a door on the left. In the left corner in the background there is a small brown table with some things on it, for example some water, a glass and a brush. Above the table there is a window. The walls of the room are blue. There are some paintings on the walls and there is a mirror next to the window. One painting above the bed on the right shows a man and the painting next to it shows a woman. There are two more paintings on the same wall but you can't see what they show. In the background there is a painting of a landscape. The person who lives in the room seems to wash himself or herself at the table because there is a towel on the wall on the left.

It is not easy to say who lives in the room. The chair next to the bed is really small, like a chair for a child. But there are no toys in the room, so I don't think that a child lives in it. There are some clothes on the wall behind the bed below the painting of the landscape. They look like a man's clothes. Perhaps the artist painted his own room.
Individuelle Ergänzungen zu interessanten oder ungewöhnlichen Details und persönliche Stellungnahme

Lass deine Punkte von deinem Lehrer/deiner Lehrerin festlegen.

☆ ___ von 10 ☾ ___ von 16 ☼ ___ von 20

T4 Writing: Your favourite music

Lösungsbeispiele:
I like German rap music, especially Cro and Sido. I think their lyrics are really cool. They know what it feels like to be young and to have lots of problems. I listen to their songs all the time and I often watch their videos on my parents' computer. I also practise speaking the lyrics and moving to them. My favourite song by Cro is … It is about … My favourite song by Sido is … In this song he sings about … I'm frustrated because I haven't been able to go to any German rap concerts. The tickets are too expensive.

I really like Taylor Swift. I often listen to her songs when I'm alone in my room. She often sings about love and problems. I understand some of the lyrics and think they are very good. I have got most of her songs on my mobile. I know some lyrics by heart and I sing along when nobody can hear me. My best friend likes the songs, too, so we often listen to them together. Taylor knows what it is like to be a teenager. I think she is a fantastic singer and she is also very beautiful. She has won lots of awards for her music.

I like metal bands. Their music gives me energy. I feel strong and free when I listen to it. Metal musicians and their fans often look wild or even dangerous with their long hair, tattoos and dark clothes, but they are usually very nice and peaceful people. At the moment my favourite band is Machine Head. They are an American band. My older brother went to one of their concerts a few years ago and said they were fantastic. I really liked them, too, and we both started listening to their songs.

Für jeden richtigen Satz erhältst du zwei Punkte.

☆ ___ von 10 ☾ ___ von 16 ☼ ___ von 20

T5 Mediation: A workshop

1. *Um einen Workshop für Graffiti und Straßenkunst*
2. *ein (professioneller Londoner) Graffitikünstler namens Jason Lacombe*
3. *Acht- bis 16-Jährige, aber auch ihre Eltern und andere Erwachsene*
4. *Jeden Samstag von 11 bis 15 Uhr*
5. *£20 für Kinder und Jugendliche, £35 für Erwachsene*
6. *Indem man ein Datum auswählt und auf* „Book now“ *klickt/unter* „Book now“ *seine Angaben macht.*

Für jede richtige Antwort erhältst du zwei Punkte.

☆ ___ von 6 ☾ ___ von 10 ☼ ___ von 12

LiF 1 Mengenangaben – *much/many/a lot of*

Much, many und *a lot of* bedeuten „viel“ bzw. „viele“ auf Deutsch. Was ist der Unterschied?

- *Many* steht vor zählbaren Nomen *(countable nouns)* im Plural, z. B. *restaurants, potatoes, apples* usw.

  *There are **many** restaurants in Notting Hill.* *There aren't **many** potatoes left.*

  Mit *how many* fragst du nach der Anzahl von Dingen:

  *How **many** restaurants are there in Notting Hill?*

- *Much* steht vor nicht zählbaren Nomen *(uncountable nouns)* im Singular, z. B. *ice cream, milk, water* usw.

  *I had so **much** ice cream!* *There isn't **much** milk in the fridge.*

  Mit *how much* fragst du nach Mengen:

  *How **much** water do you need?* *How **much** time have we got?*

- In positiven Aussagesätzen benutzt man eher *a lot of* oder auch *lots of* statt *much* und *many*. Dabei brauchst du nicht zwischen zählbaren und nicht zählbaren Nomen zu unterscheiden:

  *There was **a lot of** meat in that curry.* *There were **a lot of** potatoes on the plate.*

LiF 2R Das Perfekt – *present perfect (revision)*

Das *present perfect* verwendest du,

- wenn etwas bis zum jetzigen Zeitpunkt irgendwann, noch nie oder noch nicht geschehen ist:
  Rosemary has been to many foreign countries before, but she has never been to Italy.
- wenn ein Vorgang in der Vergangenheit noch Auswirkungen auf die Gegenwart hat:
  I've already cooked dinner, you don't have to do it!

*She **has baked** a cake. It is ready now.*

a) Aussagesätze im *present perfect*

Das *present perfect* bildest du mit *have/has* + **Partizip Perfekt *(past participle)***.
Die Verneinung bildest du mit ***haven't/hasn't*** + **Partizip Perfekt**.

*I **have cleaned** the kitchen.*
*He **has gone** to London.*
*They **have cooked** chicken curry.*

*She **hasn't been** to Scotland.*
*They **haven't finished** their homework.*

Das *present perfect* kannst du mit Adverbien der unbestimmten Zeit verwenden, z. B. mit *already, just, ever, never, yet, not yet*. Es ist in solchen Sätzen nicht wichtig, wann genau etwas geschehen ist. Die Adverbien stehen dann direkt vor dem Partizip Perfekt:

*I have **already** done my homework.* *Charlie has **just** eaten breakfast.*

! Beachte die Ausnahme: Das Wort *yet* steht am Satzende.

*I haven't been to London **yet**.*

b) Fragen und Kurzantworten im *present perfect*

Entscheidungsfragen im *present perfect* bildest du, indem du *have* oder *has* an den Satzanfang stellst.

***present perfect:* Entscheidungsfragen und Kurzantworten**

	+	–
Have you **finished** your homework? **Has** Rosemary **been** to Hong Kong?	**Yes, I have.** **Yes, she has.**	**No, I haven't.** **No, she hasn't.**

Bei Fragen mit Fragewörtern steht das Fragewort am Satzanfang:

*What **have** you **chosen**?* *Why **has** Rosemary **travelled** all over the world?*

c) Das Partizip Perfekt

Bei regelmäßigen Verben bildest du das Partizip Perfekt *(past participle)* mit dem **Infinitiv** + *-ed*.
Beachte die Besonderheiten bei der Schreibung der *ed*-Endungen (siehe auch LiF 11R).

Infinitiv	*simple past*	*past participle*
clean	cleaned	clean**ed**
cook	cooked	cook**ed**
play	played	play**ed**

Language in Focus

Unregelmäßige Verben haben besondere Formen. Lerne sie wie Vokabeln.
Auf Seite 304–306 im Textbook findest du eine Liste mit unregelmäßigen Verben.

Infinitiv	simple past	past participle
be	was/were	been
do	did	done
have	had	had
buy	bought	bought

LiF 3 Bestätigungsfragen – *question tags (optional)*

Wenn du möchtest, dass ein Gesprächspartner dir zustimmt, kannst du *question tags* verwenden.
Du kannst sie mit „oder?", „nicht wahr?" usw. übersetzen.

He is a great cook, isn't he?

The chips are delicious, aren't they?

In *question tags* werden das Verb und das Subjekt aus einer Aussage aufgegriffen. Bei positiven Aussagen wird das Verb verneint. In den Beispielen oben wird die verneinte Form von *be (isn't* bzw. *aren't)* verwendet. Dann folgt das Subjekt aus dem Aussagesatz. Ist es ein Personalpronomen, dann wird es wiederholt *(he)*. Ist es ein Nomen *(the chips)*, dann verwendet man im *question tag* das passende Personalpronomen *(they)*.

Bei Sätzen mit Modal- oder Hilfsverben verwendest du deren verneinte Form und ein Personalpronomen:

You can read Chinese, can't you?

Rajiv will make samosas, won't he?

Bei Sätzen mit Vollverben verwendest du die passende Form von *do*:

Karla likes curry, doesn't she?

You travel a lot, don't you?

LiF 4 Relativsätze – *relative clauses*

Relativsätze sind Nebensätze, die Personen oder Dinge näher beschreiben.
Ein Relativsatz beginnt meist mit einem Relativpronomen: *who*, *which* oder *that*.

Dabei verwendest du *who* für Personen und *which* für Dinge.
Das Relativpronomen *that* kannst du sowohl für Dinge als auch für Personen benutzen.

	Relativsatz
There is a man	*who is selling sports equipment.*
There is a stall	*which is selling earrings.*
We bought earrings	*that were only £4.*
There are many people	*that sell things at the car boot sale.*

Relativsätze können auch in der Mitte des Satzes stehen:

The man who is selling sports equipment has an interesting stall.

LiF 5R Die Verlaufsform der Gegenwart – *present progressive (revision)*

Das *present progressive* verwendest du, um zu sagen, was jemand gerade tut oder was gerade passiert.

a) Aussagesätze im *present progressive*
So bildest du das *present progressive:* **Form von *be (am, is, are)*** + *ing*-Form.

I am playing the steel drums.
Rajiv is selling samosas.

The children are watching the parade.

! Beachte: Endet der Infinitiv auf -e, dann fällt das -e in der *ing*-Form weg.

make → making	*Rajiv is making samosas.*
dance → dancing	*Vanessa is dancing.*

! Endet der Infinitiv auf einen kurzen betonten **Vokal + Konsonant**, dann wird der Konsonant verdoppelt.

put → putting	*Rajiv is putting food on the table.*
run → running	*Charlie is running.*

Für die Verneinung fügst du *not* hinter *am, is* oder *are* ein. Hier verwendet man oft die Kurzform:

I'm not making pizza. *David isn't dancing.* *They aren't watching TV.*

b) Fragen und Kurzantworten
Bei Entscheidungsfragen stellst du die Form von *be* an den Satzanfang. In Kurzantworten wird diese Form aufgegriffen.

Is Rajiv making samosas? – Yes, he is./No, he isn't.
Are they going to the carnival? – Yes, they are./No, they aren't.

Bei Fragen mit Fragewort stellst du das Fragewort an den Anfang:

What are you doing? *Where are you going?* *Why is David laughing?*

LiF6 Die Verlaufsform der Vergangenheit – *past progressive*

Es gibt auch für die Vergangenheit eine *progressive form*, das *past progressive*. Es drückt aus,
- was jemand zu einem bestimmten Zeitpunkt in der Vergangenheit gerade tat oder was gerade passierte.
- was gerade vor sich ging, als etwas anderes geschah.

a) Bejahte und verneinte Aussagesätze
So bildest du das *past progressive*: **simple past-Form von be (was/were)** + *ing*-Form.

Charlie was playing the steel drums.	*Charlie spielte (gerade) Steeldrums.*
The children were laughing.	*Die Kinder lachten (gerade).*

Wenn du beschreiben willst, was gerade vor sich ging, als etwas anderes geschah, kannst du das so tun:

Gillian was reading a book	when Rajiv called.
The pupils were running around	when the teacher came.

was gerade passierte: *past progressive* → neues Ereignis: *simple past*

David was playing computer games when his mum came in.

Für die Verneinung fügst du einfach *not* hinter der Form von *be* ein:

Rajiv was not reading a book. He wasn't listening to music, either.

b) Fragen und Kurzantworten
Entscheidungsfragen im *past progressive* bildest du, indem du *was* bzw. *were* an den Satzanfang stellst:

Was Rajiv laughing? – Yes, he was./No, he wasn't.
Were the children running around? – Yes, they were./No, they weren't.

Bei Fragen mit Fragewörtern stellst du das Fragewort an den Satzanfang:

What were you doing? *Where were you going?* *Why was David laughing?*

LiF7 Die *ing*-Form als Nomen – *ing-nouns*

Wird ein Verb wie ein Nomen verwendet, nennt man das Gerundium *(gerund)*.
Im Englischen benutzt du dafür die *ing*-Form des Verbs:
Dancing can be fun. – Tanzen kann Spaß machen.

- Das Gerundium kann Subjekt eines Satzes sein:

  Running keeps you fit.

- Das Gerundium folgt oft nach bestimmten Verben wie *like, love, enjoy, hate, start* und *stop*:

  She enjoys listening to music. *I like going to the cinema.*

- Du benutzt das Gerundium auch nach bestimmten Ausdrücken wie *good at* oder *bad at*:

  I'm good at playing basketball.

Achte auf die Schreibweise der *ing*-Form (siehe auch LiF 5R):

dance – dancing, run – running, hit – hitting, stop – stopping usw.

LiF8R Vergleichsformen des Adjektivs – *comparison of adjectives (revision)*

a) Steigerung von Adjektiven mit *-er* und *-est*

Einsilbige Adjektive (z. B. *tall, strong*) werden meist durch das Anhängen von *-er* und *-est* gesteigert. Auch einige zweisilbige Adjektive können mit *-er* und *-est* gesteigert werden, vor allem Adjektive, die auf *-er, -le, -ow* und *-y* enden.

Adjektiv	Komparativ	Superlativ
tall	taller	(the) tallest
strong	stronger	(the) strongest
clever	cleverer	(the) cleverest

! Bei manchen Adjektiven ändert sich die Schreibweise.

Adjektiv	Komparativ	Superlativ
nice	nicer	(the) nicest
fit	fitter	(the) fittest
simple	simpler	(the) simplest

! Bei zweisilbigen Adjektiven, die auf *-y* enden, wird *-y* zu *-i*.

Adjektiv	Komparativ	Superlativ
easy	easier	(the) easiest
friendly	friendlier	(the) friendliest

! Einige Adjektive haben unregelmäßige Steigerungsformen.

Adjektiv	Komparativ	Superlativ
good	better	(the) best
bad	worse	(the) worst

b) Steigerung von Adjektiven mit *more* und *most*

Mehrsilbige Adjektive werden mit *more* und *most* gesteigert. Du stellst dabei *more* oder *most* vor das Adjektiv. Das Adjektiv bleibt unverändert.

Adjektiv	Komparativ	Superlativ
famous	more famous	(the) most famous
successful	more successful	(the) most successful

Tom is the most successful runner.

c) Vergleichssätze

Wenn du Personen, Tiere oder Dinge miteinander vergleichst, benutzt du den Komparativ mit *than*.

Tom is faster than Jack. *Amy is more successful than Janet.*

Sind die Eigenschaften von Personen, Tieren oder Dingen gleich, benutzt du *as ... as*.

Mike is as fast as Finn. *Sarah is as successful as Anne.*

LiF9R Modalverben – *modal verbs (revision)*

Mithilfe von Modalverben kannst du zum Beispiel ausdrücken, was jemand tun kann, darf oder muss:
Mum, can I go the party? – Yes, but you must do your homework first.

a) Fähigkeit: *can/can't/be able to*

Mit *can* drückst du aus,
- was jemand tun kann
- was jemand tun darf.

He can swim. *You can watch TV.*

Can steht mit dem Infinitiv und bleibt in allen Personen gleich.

! Die Ersatzform von *can* ist *be able to*. Im *simple past* kannst du auch *could* benutzen.

The old lady isn't able to eat very much.
We aren't able to go on holiday this year.
Charlie was able to walk to the doctor's office.
Charlie couldn't move his finger.

b) Erlaubnis: *can/can't – be allowed to/not be allowed to – may/may not – must not*

Can/can't, be allowed to, may/may not und *must not* benutzt du zum Beispiel, wenn du
- um Erlaubnis fragst oder jemandem etwas erlaubst
- um etwas bittest
- etwas verbietest.

Can I swim in the pool? – Yes, you can, but you are not allowed to swim in the lake.
May I watch the film tonight?
You mustn't move your broken arm.

! *Must not* (Kurzform *mustn't*) klingt wie „muss nicht" im Deutschen, bedeutet aber „etwas nicht dürfen".

You mustn't talk now. Ihr dürft jetzt nicht sprechen.

c) Notwendigkeit: *must/have to – don't have to/needn't*

Must bedeutet „müssen". In der Regel kannst du ***must*** auch durch ***have to/has to*** ersetzen.

*Gillian **must** tidy her room. = Gillian **has to** tidy her room.*

Must hat keine eigene Vergangenheitsform. Daher wird die *simple past*-Form von ***have to*** benutzt.

*Yesterday Gillian **had to** tidy her room.*

Wenn du sagen willst, was jemand nicht tun muss, benutzt du ***don't/doesn't have to***.

*I **have to** do the washing up but I **don't have to** vacuum the floor.*

Auch mit ***needn't*** (Kurzform von ***need not***) kannst du ausdrücken, dass jemand etwas nicht tun muss.

*You **needn't** do your homework now. You can do it later.*

LiF10 Bedingungssätze 1 – *conditional 1*

Wenn du sagen willst, was unter bestimmten Bedingungen geschehen wird oder geschehen kann, benutzt du einen Bedingungssatz: *If you have a broken leg, you will get an X-ray.*

Ein Bedingungssatz besteht aus einem *if*-Satz *(if-clause)* und einem Hauptsatz *(main clause):*

- Der *if*-Satz nennt eine Bedingung. Der Hauptsatz erläutert, was passiert, wenn die Bedingung erfüllt ist.
- Im *if*-Satz steht das *simple present*, im Hauptsatz das *will-future*.

***if*-Satz**	**Hauptsatz**	
If you **miss** the bus,	you **will be** late.	*Wenn du den Bus verpasst, kommst du zu spät.*
If it **rains**,	they **won't go** outside.	*Wenn es regnet, werden sie nicht rausgehen.*

Bedingungssätze können entweder mit dem *if*-Satz oder mit dem Hauptsatz beginnen. Fangen sie mit dem *if*-Satz an, werden sie durch ein Komma getrennt. Steht der Hauptsatz vorn, verwendet man kein Komma:

If you go to the cinema, I'll come with you. *I'll come with you if you go to the cinema.*

Im Hauptsatz kannst du auch Modalverben (z. B. *can, must*) oder den Imperativ verwenden:

*If you feel sick, you **can stay** at home.* *If you need help, **ask** your teacher.*

! *If* und *when* kannst du beide mit „wenn" übersetzen. Sie werden aber unterschiedlich verwendet:

- ***If** I see Ben on Monday, I'll give him the book.* Der Sprecher verwendet *if*, weil er nicht sicher ist, ob er Ben am Montag sieht. Du kannst *if* hier mit „wenn" oder „falls" übersetzen.
- ***When** I see Ben on Monday, I'll give him the book.* Der Sprecher weiß, dass er Ben am Montag sehen und ihm das Buch geben wird. Du kannst *when* hier mit „wenn" übersetzen, aber nicht mit „falls".

LiF11R Die einfache Vergangenheit – *simple past (revision)*

Das *simple past* verwendest du, wenn du über etwas sprechen willst, das in der Vergangenheit liegt und abgeschlossen ist, zum Beispiel wenn du berichtest, was du erlebt hast, oder wenn du eine Geschichte erzählst: *Robinson Crusoe left his parents and boarded a ship to London. He …*

a) Regelmäßige Formen

Das *simple past* der regelmäßigen Verben bildest du, indem du die Endung *-ed* an den Infinitiv anhängst:

board + -ed → boarded *He boarded a ship.*

We played football on Thursday. *Last Sunday I watched a film.*

! Achte auf folgende Besonderheiten in der Rechtschreibung: Endet das Verb auf *-e*, dann wird nur *-d* angehängt. *like → liked*

Endet das Verb auf einen kurzen betonten **Vokal + Konsonant**, wird der Konsonant verdoppelt. *stop → stopped*

Endet das Verb auf **Konsonant + *-y***, dann lautet die Endung im *simple past* *-ied*. *tidy → tidied*

b) Unregelmäßige Formen

Unregelmäßige Verben haben im *simple past* eigene Formen, die du lernen musst.

Infinitiv	*simple past*
leave	left
go	went
hit	hit

*Robinson **left** his parents.* *He **went** on board.* *The ship **hit** some rocks.*

Be hat als einziges Verb zwei Formen im *simple past*, **was** und **were**:

*I/he/she/it **was** – you/we/they **were***

Du verneinst diese Formen, indem du einfach ***not*** anhängst.

*Robinson **was** alone for many years.*
*It **wasn't** cold on the island.*

*Robinson and Man Friday **were** back in York in 1687.*
*They **weren't** at home.*

Entscheidungsfragen mit *be* im *simple past* bildest du, indem du ***was/were*** an den Satzanfang stellst:

__Was__ the island beautiful? – ***Yes it was./No, it wasn't.***
__Were__ you two alone on the island? – ***Yes, we were./No, we weren't.***

Bei Fragen mit Fragewort steht das Fragewort am Satzanfang: *__How__ was the weather?*

c) Verneinung mit *didn't*

Vollverben im *simple past* (außer *be*) verneinst du mit ***didn't (did not)***. Das Verb selbst bleibt im Infinitiv.

*Robinson **didn't talk** to Friday.* *I **didn't go** to London.*

d) Entscheidungsfragen mit *did*

Entscheidungsfragen im *simple past* stellst du mit *did*:

__Did__ you __go__ to London? – ***Yes, I did./No, I didn't.***
__Did__ Robinson __miss his__ parents? – ***Yes, he did./No, he didn't.***

e) Fragen mit Fragewort und *did*

Das Fragewort steht auch hier am Satzanfang:

__How did__ Robinson __teach__ Man Friday English? *__What did__ Robinson __do__?*

LiF12 Die Stellung der Satzglieder – *word order*

a) Satzstellung Subjekt – Verb – Objekt (S – V – O)

Im englischen Aussagesatz ist die Satzstellung meist Subjekt – Verb – Objekt (S – V – O):

Subjekt	Verb	Objekt
Robinson	left	his parents.
He	built	a raft.

b) Aussagesätze mit Häufigkeitsadverbien

Häufigkeitsadverbien *(adverbs of frequency)* stehen meist zwischen Subjekt und Verb:

Subjekt	Häufigkeitsadverb	Verb	
I	often	missed	my home.
Robinson	never	gave up.	

! Häufigkeitsadverbien stehen jedoch hinter den Formen von *be* und hinter *can*:

*It was **always** very hot on the island.* *You can **sometimes** find fresh water on a lonely island.*

c) Ortsangaben und Zeitangaben

Orts- und Zeitangaben stehen in der Regel am Satzende. Hierbei gilt „Ort vor Zeit".

	Ortsangabe	Zeitangabe
Robinson Crusoe lived	on the island	for many years.
He and Man Friday arrived	in York	on 11 June 1687.

Um eine Zeitangabe zu betonen, stellt man sie an den Satzanfang. Das gilt auch für Häufigkeitsadverbien.

Zeitangabe		Ortsangabe
In 1659	a British ship sailed by.	
Sometimes	Robinson was lonely	on the island.

LiF 13 Bedingungssätze 2 – conditional 2 (optional)

- Bedingungssätze können realistische oder unrealistische Bedingungen nennen (siehe LiF10).

  If you call your friend, you will make him happy

  Hier ist die Bedingung erfüllbar, denn die Person braucht den Freund nur anzurufen.

  If I had an aunt in London, I would visit her and go on to the London Eye.

  Wer das sagt, hat keine Tante in London, sonst würde er oder sie anders reden. Die Bedingung für einen solchen Besuch in London ist also nicht erfüllbar – die Idee bleibt eine Wunschvorstellung.

- Mit einem Bedingungssatz kannst du also auch ausdrücken, was unter einer nur gedachten Bedingung passieren würde oder könnte. Oft geht es dabei um Ereignisse, die unwahrscheinlich oder unmöglich sind:

  If I had a lot of money, I would go to Australia.

- Bei dieser zweiten Art von Bedingungssätzen steht der *if*-Satz im *simple past*. Im Hauptsatz steht *would* oder auch *could*. Danach folgt ein Verb im Infinitiv.

if-Satz	Hauptsatz		
If I had a friend in Australia,	I	would could	visit her.

- Bei *if*-Sätzen heißt es manchmal *If I were* ..., aber du kannst auch *If I was* ... sagen. Beide Formen sind hier möglich.

  If I were rich, I would buy a fast car. Oder: *If I was rich, I would buy a fast car.*

LiF14 Das Passiv – *the passive*

Aktivsätze sagen uns, wer oder was handelt. Wenn es aber unwichtig oder unklar ist, wer etwas tut oder getan hat, kannst du das Passiv verwenden.

Das Passiv bildest du so: Form von *be* + **Partizip Perfekt *(past participle)***

Passiv im *simple present:*
English is spoken all over the world.
Matches are used to make fire.

Passiv im *simple past:*
My computer was made in China.
These books were written in Germany.

Wenn du in einem Passivsatz doch einmal die handelnde Person oder die Ursache für etwas nennen willst, hängst du sie mit *by* („von", „durch") an den Satz an:

The first car was invented by Karl Benz. *The house was destroyed by fire.*

LiF15 Indirekte Rede 1 – *reported speech 1*

Wenn du berichten willst, was jemand gesagt hat, benutzt du indirekte Rede.

- Indirekte Rede besteht aus einem Begleitsatz und der wiedergegebenen Aussage. Beide Satzteile können, müssen aber nicht unbedingt durch *that* verbunden werden.

	Begleitsatz	wiedergegebene Aussage
"We could do with a break."	*Sabrina says (that)*	*they could do with a break.*
"It was fantastic."	*Gillian says (that)*	*it was fantastic.*

- Wenn der Begleitsatz in der Gegenwart steht, verändern sich die Zeiten in der wiedergegebenen Aussage nicht.
- Wenn die Originalaussage Wörter enthält, die nur aus dem Zusammenhang richtig zu verstehen sind, musst du sie in der wiedergegebenen Aussage anpassen:

  "I'm tired." *Gillian says (that) she's tired.*

Liebe Schülerin, lieber Schüler,

hier findest du Portfolio-Fragebögen. Darin notierst du, was du schon alles kannst. So hast du die Möglichkeit, eigenständig festzustellen, welche Fortschritte du machst.

Fülle die Fragebögen jedes Mal aus, wenn ihr ein *Theme* im Textbook und Workbook abgeschlossen habt.

Das geht so:

Sieh dir zum Beispiel die Sätze unter „Hören" an. Lies sie und überlege, wie gut du das kannst, was dort beschrieben ist.

Hinter jedem Satz steht, wo du nachschlagen kannst, wenn du nicht genau weißt, was gemeint ist. Du kannst die Übungen auch gleich noch einmal wiederholen, wenn du noch nicht richtig fit bist. Falls ihr im Unterricht nicht alle Übungen gemacht habt, kannst du den betreffenden Satz überspringen.

Vor jedem Satz steht ein Kreis. ◯

Wenn du meinst, dass du etwas schon gut kannst, dann male den Kreis grün aus. ●

Dir fällt etwas noch schwer?
Dann male den Kreis gelb aus. ●
Lies anschließend die angegebene Stelle im Textbook (TB) oder Workbook (WB) nach.

Wenn du feststellst, dass du etwas noch nicht kannst, male den Kreis rot aus. ●
Sieh dir die passende Stelle im TB oder WB noch einmal ganz genau an und wiederhole die Übung.

Auf der letzten Seite findest du einen Fragebogen, auf dem du am Ende der Klasse 7 abhaken kannst, was dir am besten beim Englischlernen geholfen hat.

Und jetzt: Viel Spaß!

Hören 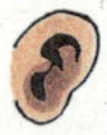

Das kann ich noch nicht.

Das fällt mir noch schwer.

Das kann ich gut.

- ◯ Ich verstehe, was Gäste im Restaurant bestellen. (TB A4)
- ◯ Ich kann einem Dialog bestimmte Informationen entnehmen. (TB A7, A10, B1c)

Lesen 

- ◯ Ich kann Speisekarten größtenteils verstehen. (TB A3)
- ◯ Ich kann einem Dialog wichtige Informationen entnehmen. (TB A7c, B1)
- ◯ Ich verstehe die Anweisungen in einem Rezept. (TB B5)
- ◯ Ich kann kurzen Informationstexten, zum Beispiel über Nahrungsgewohnheiten in unterschiedlichen Ländern, wichtige Informationen entnehmen. (TB B9a)

Sprechen

- ◯ Ich kann über verschiedene Nahrungsmittel und Gerichte sprechen. (TB A1, A3)
- ◯ Ich kann eine Rolle in einem Dialog im Restaurant spielen. (TB A11)
- ◯ Ich kann einen kurzen Vortrag über ein bekanntes Thema halten. (TB B11)

Schreiben 

- ◯ Ich kann kurze Informationstexte für eine Präsentation verfassen. (TB B11)

Sprachmittlung 

- ◯ Ich kann Informationen aus einer Restaurantkritik auf Deutsch wiedergeben. (TB A9)
- ◯ Ich kann in einem Restaurant beim Bestellen sprachlich aushelfen. (WB A7)

Wortschatz

- ◯ Ich kenne Bezeichnungen für unterschiedliche Nahrungsmittel, Gewürze, Zutaten und Gerichte. (TB A3, B1, B5)

Lern- und Arbeitstechniken

- ◯ Ich kann Grammatikregeln aus Beispielen in einem Text ableiten. (TB A8)
- ◯ Ich kann beim Hören von Informationen Notizen machen und anschließend darüber sprechen. (TB B9c)
- ◯ Ich kann mich einbringen, wenn wir in einer Gruppe eine Präsentation vorbereiten. (TB B11)

Außerdem kann ich jetzt Folgendes:

____

Hören

○ Ich kann einem Videoclip bestimmte Aussagen entnehmen. (TB A2)

○ Ich kann einem Dialog bestimmte Aussagen entnehmen. (TB A4, A10, B12)

○ Ich kann nach dem ersten Hören sagen, worum es in einem Lied geht. (TB B4)

Lesen

○ Ich kann eine Handlung zusammenfassen, zum Beispiel die Handlung des Musicals *The Lion King.* (TB A9)

○ Ich kann Texten die wichtigsten Informationen entnehmen, zum Beispiel Blogs und einem Zeitungsartikel. (TB B5, B8, B10)

Sprechen

○ Ich kann über mögliche Aktivitäten und besondere Ereignisse in meiner Heimatregion sprechen. (TB A1, A11)

○ Ich kann eine Rolle in einem Verkaufsdialog spielen. (TB A8)

○ Ich kann Fotos beschreiben, zum Beispiel vom Notting Hill Carnival. (TB B1c)

○ Ich kann beschreiben, was in der Vergangenheit gerade passierte. (TB B11)

Schreiben

○ Ich kann über ein Straßenfest schreiben. (TB B6a)

○ Ich kann einen Beitrag zu einem Klassenprodukt verfassen, zum Beispiel über den Notting Hill Carnival. (TB B13)

Sprachmittlung

○ Ich kann auf Deutsch wiedergeben, worum es auf einem Informationsposter geht, zum Beispiel in einem Warnhinweis. (TB B9d)

Wortschatz

○ Ich kann bekannten und neuen Wortschatz zu einem Thema zusammenstellen, zum Beispiel zum Oberbegriff *carnival.* (TB B1b, B7 2.)

Lern- und Arbeitstechniken

○ Ich kann beim Lesen Notizen machen und anschließend darüber sprechen. (TB A9c)

○ Ich kann einen Text, den ich geschrieben habe, zusammen mit einem Partner/einer Partnerin überarbeiten. (TB B6b)

○ Ich kann bei der Erstellung eines Klassenprodukts Vorschläge einbringen und darüber diskutieren. (TB B13)

Außerdem kann ich jetzt Folgendes:

Hören

- ◯ Ich kann verstehen, worum es in einem Dialog geht. (TB A9)
- ◯ Ich kann einem Dialog eine bestimmte einzelne Information entnehmen. (TB B1b)

Lesen

- ◯ Ich kann einem Dialog entnehmen, worum es geht. (TB B1a)
- ◯ Ich kann einem Text bestimmte Informationen entnehmen, zum Beispiel einer Lebensgeschichte. (TB B9)

Sprechen

- ◯ Ich kann über Sportler, Sportlerinnen und Mannschaften sprechen. (TB A7, A8b)
- ◯ Ich kann Vergleiche formulieren (TB A8a)
- ◯ Ich kann sagen, was unter bestimmten Bedingungen passieren wird. (TB B5)

Schreiben

- ◯ Ich kann über eine Sportart schreiben, die ich ausübe oder mir gern ansehe. (TB A5)
- ◯ Ich kann über eine Krankheit schreiben. (TB B4b)
- ◯ Ich kann einen Text über eine Situation im Wartezimmer schreiben, zum Beispiel einen Comic, einen Dialog, eine Geschichte oder eine E-Mail. (TB B11)

Sprachmittlung

- ◯ Ich kann einer britischen Person beim Arztbesuch in Deutschland sprachlich aushelfen. (TB B7)

Wortschatz

- ◯ Ich kenne eine Reihe von Wörtern und Ausdrücken zum Thema Sport. (TB A1, A7)
- ◯ Ich kenne eine Reihe von Wörtern und Ausdrücken, mit denen ich über Krankheiten und Beschwerden sprechen kann. (TB B2, B4a)

Lern- und Arbeitstechniken

- ◯ Ich kann meine Ideen zu einem Projekt erläutern und mit anderen über unsere unterschiedlichen Vorschläge diskutieren. (TB A10)
- ◯ Ich kann Wörter und Ausdrücke im Wörterbuch nachschlagen. (TB B1d)

Außerdem kann ich jetzt Folgendes:

___

Hören 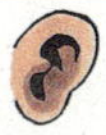

○ Ich kann Details in einem Dialog verstehen. (TB A5)

Lesen 

○ Ich kann einen Comic verstehen. (TB A1)

○ Ich kann kurze Texte zusammenfassen, zum Beispiel Briefe und Antworten auf einer Kummerkastenseite. (TB B2b)

○ Ich verstehe Details in einem Erzähltext. (TB B4)

Sprechen 

○ Ich kann über den Nutzen bestimmter Dinge sprechen. (TB A11)

○ Ich kann meine Meinung äußern, wenn ich Formulierungshilfen habe. (TB B3c)

○ Ich kann in einem Rollenspiel frei sprechen, wenn ich meine Rolle vorher intensiv geübt habe. (TB B9)

Schreiben 

○ Ich kann eine Geschichte nacherzählen. (TB A4)

○ Ich kann einen Ratschlag formulieren. (TB B3d)

Sprachmittlung 

○ Ich kann Informationen, die ich auf Deutsch gehört habe, auf Englisch wiedergeben. (TB P16)

○ Ich kann Sprichwörter sinngemäß auf Englisch wiedergeben. (WB A7)

Wortschatz 

○ Ich kenne eine Reihe von Wörtern, mit denen ich Gefühle beschreiben kann. (TB A2, B1)

○ Ich kann ein Wortnetz mit bekanntem und neuem Wortschatz erstellen, zum Beispiel zum Thema *home* oder über Charlies Familie. (TB A9a, B6 1.)

Lern- und Arbeitstechniken

○ Ich kann dazu beitragen, dass wir uns bei der Gruppenarbeit auf bestimmte Punkte einigen. (TB A11)

○ Ich kann Ideen zu einem Rollenspiel beitragen und gemeinsam mit anderen Gruppenmitgliedern ausarbeiten. (TB B9)

Außerdem kann ich jetzt Folgendes:

____

Hören

◯ Ich kann einem Dialog bestimmte Details entnehmen. (TB A2c)

◯ Ich verstehe Texte gut, wenn ich sie gleichzeitig beim Lesen höre. (TB B2d)

◯ Ich kann einem Videoclip gezielt Informationen entnehmen. (TB A7a)

Lesen

◯ Ich verstehe die wichtigsten Informationen in Sachtexten, zum Beispiel in einem Museumsprospekt oder in Texten über Erfindungen. (TB A1, B2, B3)

◯ Ich verstehe die wichtigsten Aussagen in einem Blogeintrag. (TB A6)

Sprechen

◯ Ich kann einen flüssigen Kurzvortrag halten, wenn ich ihn vorher einige Male geübt habe. (TB A8)

◯ Ich kann mich mit anderen darüber austauschen, welche Gegenstände und Geräte im Alltag wichtig für uns sind. (TB B1)

◯ Ich kann zusammenhängend über einige Erfindungen sprechen. (TB B8b, B10)

Schreiben

◯ Ich kann mir Notizen zu einem Text machen und mit ihnen anschließend einen eigenen Text schreiben. (TB B3b, c, WB B2)

◯ Ich kann zusammen mit anderen in einer Gruppe Anleitungen für ein technisches Gerät schreiben. (TB B10 7.)

Sprachmittlung

◯ Ich kann mithilfe gezielter Fragen auf Deutsch wiedergeben, was in einer Tonaufnahme gesagt wird. (TB P3)

Wortschatz

◯ Ich kenne Wörter und Ausdrücke, mit denen ich über Erfindungen sprechen kann. (TB B1, B7)

◯ Ich kenne Formulierungen, mit denen ich den anderen in meiner Klasse nach einer Präsentation faires Feedback geben kann. (TB B10 8.)

Lern- und Arbeitstechniken

◯ Ich kann vor dem Hören oder Lesen eines Texts anhand der Überschrift oder der Bilder Vermutungen äußern, worum es wohl geht. (TB A2)

◯ Ich kann Grammatikregeln aus Beispielen ableiten und mithilfe des LiF-Teils überprüfen, ob ich sie richtig formuliert habe. (TB B4)

Außerdem kann ich jetzt Folgendes:

____

Hören

- ◯ Ich verstehe Tonaufnahmen so gut, dass ich mir beim Hören Notizen machen kann. (TB B3d)

Lesen

- ◯ Ich kann Belege aus einem Text angeben, wenn ich Fragen zum Leseverstehen beantworte. (TB A2b)
- ◯ Ich verstehe wichtige Details in Informationstexten, auch wenn sie neue Fachausdrücke enthalten. (TB A3)
- ◯ Ich erfasse, wer in einem Dialog welche Aussagen von sich gibt. (TB A2c, A3c, B2b)

Sprechen

- ◯ Ich kann meine Meinung formulieren und begründen. (TB A1, B3c)
- ◯ Ich kann zusammenhängend über Musiker und Musikerinnen, Bands, Konzerte oder Songs sprechen. (TB A7 2., 4. und 5.)
- ◯ Ich kann mich mit anderen in meiner Klasse über verschiedene Themen austauschen und dabei mehr als einmal etwas sagen. (TB A1b, B1b, B3c)

Schreiben

- ◯ Ich kann Texte verfassen, die zu einem Produkt passen, zum Beispiel zu einem Poster oder einer Zeitschrift. (TB A7 1. und 3.)
- ◯ Ich kann eine Geschichte oder ein Gedicht zu einem Thema schreiben. (TB B9 1. und 2.)

Sprachmittlung

- ◯ Ich kann Angaben aus kurzen Informationstexten vom Englischen ins Deutsche oder umgekehrt vom Deutschen ins Englische übertragen. (TB P7, WB B1)
- ◯ Ich kann Erläuterungen, die ich zu einem Kunstwerk höre, sinngemäß auf Englisch wiedergeben. (TB P10)

Wortschatz

- ◯ Ich kenne viele Wörter und Ausdrücke zum Thema Musik. (TB A1, A3)
- ◯ Ich kenne Wörter und Ausdrücke, mit denen ich Kunstwerke beschreiben kann. (TB B3; WB B2, B3)

Lern- und Arbeitstechniken

- ◯ Ich kann eigenständig entscheiden, welches Produkt ich am besten für eine Zielaufgabe erstellen möchte. (TB A7, B9)
- ◯ Ich kenne unterschiedliche Methoden, mit denen ich meine Ergebnisse in interessanter Weise präsentieren kann. (TB B9)

Außerdem kann ich jetzt Folgendes:

____

Was mir in Klasse 7 beim Englischlernen geholfen hat:

Hören

Hörtexte verstehe ich am besten, wenn ich

- [ ] vorher schon eine Idee habe, worum es gehen könnte.
- [ ] den Text mitlesen kann.
- [ ] mir beim Hören Notizen mache.
- [ ] dazu Bilder sehe.
- [ ] ______________________

Sprechen

Sprechen fällt mir leicht, wenn ich

- [ ] einen Dialog mit einem Partner/einer Partnerin führe.
- [ ] mir vorher Notizen mache.
- [ ] etwas auswendig vortrage, zum Beispiel Reime.
- [ ] viel über ein Thema gelesen habe.
- [ ] ______________________

Lesen

Lesetexte verstehe ich am besten, wenn ich

- [ ] vor dem Lesen Bilder und Überschriften ansehe.
- [ ] mir vorher überlegt habe, worum es in dem Text wahrscheinlich geht.
- [ ] den Text mit einem Partner/einer Partnerin besprechen kann.
- [ ] meine Gedanken zu dem Text aufschreibe.
- [ ] ______________________

Schreiben

Schreiben gelingt mir am besten, wenn ich

- [ ] mich an eine Vorlage oder einen Mustertext halte.
- [ ] mir erst einmal Notizen mache.
- [ ] meinen Text durchsehen und bearbeiten kann.
- [ ] ______________________

Sprachmittlung

Das sprachliche Aushelfen gelingt mir, wenn ich

- [ ] mich auf die wichtigsten Informationen konzentriere.
- [ ] einfache, kurze Sätze formuliere.
- [ ] zusätzlich Gesten einsetze.
- [ ] ______________________

Wortschatz

Wörter lerne ich am besten, wenn ich

- [ ] sie nach Oberbegriffen sortiere.
- [ ] sie oft laut spreche.
- [ ] sie häufig wiederhole.
- [ ] einen Satz dazu schreibe.
- [ ] ______________________

Das habe ich in diesem Jahr besonders gern gemacht:

____

____

____